Celebrate the Harvest

*A Guide to the Spiritual Needs
and Religious Life of Older Adults*

DEACON WILLIAM BELL

 FriesenPress

One Printers Way
Altona, MB R0G 0B0
Canada

www.friesenpress.com

ISBN
978-1-03-913285-6 (Hardcover)
978-1-03-913284-9 (Paperback)
978-1-03-913286-3 (eBook)

1. Social Science, Gerontology

Distributed to the trade by The Ingram Book Company

For the unlearned,
old age is winter;
for the learned it is
the season of the harvest.
The Talmud

Table of Contents

For ease of reference, the source text for scripture quotations appears as a footnote when it is first cited in each chapter.

Dedication: To my wife, Wendy, whose unwavering faith and belief in me provided the confidence to mark writing this text as complete on my bucket list, and whose unceasing love and friendship made the dry times bearable and the productive times gratifying.

Preface

It was a cold and blustery Friday evening in the dead of winter. I had just arrived home from work, and my family was sitting down to supper when the telephone rang. It was my urologic oncologist, so I left the table to speak with him. It had been a couple of weeks since my tests had been completed. Why was he calling me at this time of day? It must not be good news.

The conversation was brief. He said, *"Your tests are back. You have grade 3 cancer; two cancer growths in your body. I'll need to see you in a few weeks. Call my receptionist on Monday to book an appointment. In the meantime, you might want to get yourself a book to read about cancer treatment options."*

That was it. He hung up, and I was left sitting in my living room, phone in hand, in total disbelief as to what I had just heard.

What had he said? That I had grade 3 cancer? I knew that stage 3 meant that the tumour had broken through the outside layer of the prostate gland, and it was attacking nearby organs. That made sense, because the surgeon had said that I had two growths. That must mean that the cancer had metastasized and was spreading through my body. Perhaps it was too late for any real treatment. Maybe that was why the specialist had been so distant, detaching himself from my situation.

How much time did I have left to put my affairs in order? And, right here and now, what was I going to tell my family? How was I going to tell my family? I had left the table in the middle of my children talking about their day and a room filled with laughter. Our kitchen had gone quiet when my family realized that it was the surgeon on the other end of the telephone line. The room was still silent; they were waiting, hopefully, for me to return with good news.

What I would say in the next few minutes and how I would say it was going to forever change their worlds. My attitude about my prospects for the future was going to forever change my world.

And so, I sat there in shock, phone in hand, not knowing whether to just sit there or to return to the kitchen; not knowing what to tell my family when I returned to the supper table. The moment of indecision passed when my wife, Wendy, called gently, *"Come and talk with us, honey."*

My walk to the door of death began that cold and blustery winter evening. It took me on a journey—a practical one—about what I needed to do to prepare, to tie up loose ends, to say goodbye, and to have my wife and our children positioned as well as possible to go on without me. It took me on both an emotional and a spiritual journey that brought me face-to-face with my own mortality.

Death is an unavoidable part of the cycle of life. Coming to terms with our mortality is a challenge that each of us will face. Accepting our mortality can help us to live more fully in the here and now, to cherish every moment of the life we have. Accepting our mortality can also be a catalyst to create something that will outlast us, touch lives that will outlive us, and experience the places and things we'd always filed away in our mind's "someday" drawer. When we recognize that life is finite, we can finally get life right. We can begin to live like we mean it.

We read in sacred Scripture, where the prophet Jeremiah delivers the Lord's message, saying:

> For surely, I know the plans I have for you, says the Lord, plans for your welfare and not for harm, to give you a future with hope. Then when you call upon me and come and pray to me, I will hear you. When you search for me, you will find me; if you seek me with all your heart ... (Jeremiah 29:11–13).[1]

As it turned out, my despair was short-lived (relatively speaking). As a Christian, I believe that there is a purpose and meaning to every life, from the baby who tragically lives just a few minutes to the great-grandmother who celebrates her 100th birthday. So, I refused to accept death as my constant companion throughout whatever life I had remaining.

In retrospect, it was a miracle in and of itself that my doctor had found the cancer growths in the first place. I had gone to my primary care physician for an annual checkup. No particular reason, but it was that time of year. During his examination, the physician had asked the right questions. And, as a result, he ordered a renal ultrasound.

It was the renal ultrasound that found a tumour on the wall of my bladder, and a second independent tumour in my prostate. It was that

---

1   Holy Bible: New Revised Standard Version. (1993). Catholic Bible Press.

ultrasound, and a family physician who listened to what his patient might not be saying that put me on the path to a couple of surgeries, a change in nutritional lifestyle, a personal experience with (and a deep respect for) Eastern medicine, and now, nine years cancer-free.

In the 2007 film *The Bucket List,* Jack Nicholson and Morgan Freeman enact the characters of two men who both know they are dying of terminal illnesses. In the film, the men run away from hospital to fulfil ambitions on their individual bucket lists, which include activities such as skydiving and flying over the North Pole. Before long, the two men find themselves talking about life's big questions, such as God and whether there is life after death.

As for my personal bucket list, I decided to stop putting off for another day and, instead, to get on with writing this text about approaching the harvest season of our lives.

Chapter One

How Old Is Old?

It has been said that *"beauty is in the eye of the beholder."* While that may well be true, a U.S. Trust study[2] found that perceptions of the onset of old age vary widely among different generations.[3] It seems that old age, too, may be in the eye of the beholder. The study reported that millennials (respondents between 18 and 32 years of age) were of the view that you are old once you turn 59 years of age. Gen Xers (respondents aged 33 to 48) held a slightly more generous view, saying that old age begins at 65 years. When it came to baby boomers (respondents aged 49 to 67 years) and the silent generation (respondents aged 68 and older), both agreed that you're not old until you hit 73 years of age.

Other findings in the 2017 U.S. Trust Insights on Wealth & Worth report included:

---

2   U.S. Trust. (2013). *2013 U.S. Trust Insights on Wealth and Worth.* https://theestateplanningsource.com/wp-content/uploads/2014/03/UST-Key-Findings-Report-Insights-on-Wealth-and-Worth-2013.pdf.

3   For purposes of generational groupings, the study defined millennials as those respondents between 18 and 32 years of age; Generation X encompassed respondents aged 33 to 48 years; while baby boomers were defined as those respondents aged 49 to 67 years; and the silent generation included those 68 years of age and older.

- When asked the age at which a person reaches the prime of life, considering factors such as resources, potential, capacity, and influence, millennials put the age at 36 years. Gen Xers cited age 47 as the prime of one's life, while boomers and the silent generation said 50 and 52, respectively.

- When asked about youth, millennials said it ends at age 40. Both Gen Xers and boomers took a different view, believing youth is all over by age 31. When it came to the silent generation, they said that youth ends at 35 years of age.

Previous surveys have also asked respondents about their perceptions of aging. In 2009, for example, a Pew Research Center report[4] found that those under 30 believed that old age hits before a person turns 60 years of age. Middle-aged respondents cited 70 as the start of old age, while those 65 and older put the number closer to 74 years of age. If you average all of the responses, the collective answer suggests that old age begins at 68.

It shouldn't come as a surprise that the older people get, the longer they think it takes for a person to reach old age. On the lighter side, comedian Bob Hope told us that, *"You know that you are getting older when the candles cost more than the cake."* My point is that, these days, it seems that the definition of old age is that it is just a number, and whether you are old or not is determined more by how you are feeling physically and mentally than some arbitrary count of years. Rather than *"being put out to pasture,"* advancing years brings with it a series of significant life changes, such as retirement, change

---

4   PEW Research Centre. (2009). *Growing Old in America: Expectations vs. Reality.* https://www.pewresearch.org/wp-content/uploads/sites/3/2010/10/Getting-Old-in-America.pdf.

of residence, etc., which need to be embraced, not feared. Zayn Malik[5], British musician and singer, said it this way: *"There comes a day when you realize that turning the page is the best feeling in the world, because there is so much more to this book called life than just the chapter that you are reading."*

In 2015, the World Economic Forum (WEF) looked at old age through a lens which heretofore had not been considered to any great degree. The WEF defined old age through a new measure called *"prospective age,"* which looked at the average number of years people have left to live. So, according to WEF, being old doesn't start at age 65. Rather, through WEF's lens, old age begins when you have an average of 15 more years left to live.

The COVID-19 pandemic was, and continues to be, particularly dangerous for adults aged 70 and over. For example, as of March 16, 2020, the case fatality rates showed a 19.2% death rate for those aged 80 years or older who contracted the disease. This rate was, by far, the highest for any age grouping of individuals who contracted the virus. In comparison, at that time, the case fatality rate for those aged 70 to 79 years was 11.8%; for 60 to 69 years it was 3.2%; for 50 to 59 years it was 1%; and a 0.2% death rate existed for those aged 30 to 39 years. The case fatality rate for those under the age of 29 years was zero percent. Clearly, older adults were particularly susceptible to the effects of this pandemic.

Despite this clear and present danger for older adults, in the first weeks following the appearance of COVID-19 in Canada, there seemed to be a growing and repulsively ageist phrase on Facebook and other media that referred to the disease as the *"Boomer*

---

5   https://www.goodreads.com/author/quotes/5766163.Zayn_Malik

Remover." Even our respected CTV National News used this phrase "*Boomer Remover*" on occasion, as if it was nothing more than a cute colloquialism.

For some, this insensitive and inappropriate term may have suggested nothing more than that the disease was seen as placing older adults particularly at risk. Peel the layers off the onion, however, and it becomes alarmingly clear that this kind of ageist talk and ageist thinking leads all too easily to prejudicial attitudes, discriminatory practices, and institutional policies that support social institutions and governments at all levels—federal, provincial, and municipal—in placing the needs of older adults well below the needs of other age groups in the population. This mindset then becomes socially accepted and supports decision-makers in denying older adults equitable access to required emergency and life-saving health care, government support for lost investments as a result of panicked and failing market investments (as we saw only too well with the COVID-19 pandemic), and the list goes on.

As identified in the opening paragraph of this chapter, the definition of "*old*" differs depending on the age of the person being asked. After all is said and done, if a 95-year-old Finnish woman can be one of the oldest persons to bungee jump,[6] or an 80-year-old man can be the oldest person to reach the summit of Mount Everest (even after four open-heart surgeries and suffering a shattered pelvis),[7] should

---

6   Bloom, D. (2020, March 14). Brave 95-year-old is thought to be world's oldest woman to bungee jump after ignoring organiser's warnings that it could KILL her. *Daily Mail.* https://www.dailymail.co.uk/news/article-2719013/Brave-95-year-old-thought-world-s-oldest-woman-bungee-jump-ignoring-organiser-s-warnings-KILL-her.html

7   Malm, S. (2020, March 14). Eldest Conqueror of Mount Everest at the top. *Daily Mail.* https://www.dailymail.co.uk/video/news/video-1009162/Eldest-conquerer-Mount-Everest-summit.html

who we are and who we are called to be corral us in by the perceptions of others? I hardly think so.

Governments, social planners, and gerontologists have recognized the diversity of old age by defining subgroups, which enables a more accurate portrayal of significant life changes. A common but arbitrary set of subgroupings are the young-old (65 to 74 years of age); the middle-old (75 to 84 years of age) and the old-old (85 years of age and older). The division of old age into three periods highlights the reality that older adulthood can extend for thirty years or more, beginning at age sixty-five. Over that thirty-year-plus span, the wants and needs of the older individual will change.

At the risk of compartmentalizing, the needs of the young-old, recently retired and for the most part in good health, tend to be controlled by their dreams (their bucket list) and interests (e.g., hobbies, travel, climate, family), rather than by physical concerns. Although retired, this subgroup often remains active in the work force on a part-time, consulting, or volunteer basis.

The next subgroup, the middle-old, tend to be more influenced by health, safety, and frailty concerns and issues.

The third subgroup, the old-old, are more likely to require assistance with the activities of daily living and living independently.

Interwoven with the variations in physical needs and abilities of these three subgroups are the challenges imposed by dwindling disposable income and the increasing need for community as spouses and friends pass away.

Despite these somewhat stereotypical categorizations, the good news is that our world is constantly changing. Our aging population is no exception. Unlike their parents' generation and their grandparents' generation, older adults of today and tomorrow are and will be a generation with very different characteristics. They exercise twice as much as previous generations. No bocce ball or table tennis; no rocking chairs or vegetating in the desert sun.

They will continue to bike, hike, swim, sail, and ski; even play softball and basketball. They'll move to the mountains, beaches, islands, college towns... wherever the physical and intellectual action is. Studies show that at least half of today's older adults expect to work at least part time after they retire. And they'll have offices in their homes; offices with high-speed internet connections for those two or more computers, which 40 percent of them already own.

Still, many older adults will also face a growing and continuous challenge, that of maintaining their precious independence. According to the American Association for Retired Persons, 9 out of 10 older adults prefer to grow old in their own homes. Successful "aging in place" demands that one's home is equipped to support one's functional limitations and enhance one's quality of living. Refusing to be stigmatized by living in a "home for the aged" or using "elderly products," aging baby boomers will seek out designs that accommodate rather than discriminate, sympathize rather than stigmatize, and appeal to users of all ages and abilities.

At its most primal level, however, our definition of old age probably won't change all that much. Popular mythology to the contrary, our expectation of how old one needs to be in order to be thought of as an older adult has changed very little over the centuries. In sacred

Scripture, the author of Psalm 90 described the length of life as *"seventy years, or perhaps eighty, if we are strong; even then their span is only toil and trouble; they are soon gone, and we fly away"* (Psalm 90: 10).[8] And, here we are, three thousand years later in pretty much the same situation. We are considered to have reached old age when we are about 70 or 80 years of age.

There is a virtual gold mine to be dredged in the above-noted verse from sacred Scripture. So, as we close this discussion about defining older adulthood, let's go in search of gold. We'll start with a brief introduction to the art and the science of spiritual numerology. We read, *"this God, His way is perfect; the promise of the Lord proves true..."* (Psalm 18:30). All God's ways are perfect. His works are perfect and His words are perfect. Can there also be perfection in His use of numbers? The Jewish faithful of the Old Testament and the Jewish Christians of the New Testament believed that to be true. So did our Church Fathers including St. Jerome, St. Augustine, and Pope St. Gregory the Great, all of whom wrote extensively about God's plan of salvation as evidenced in His use of numbers.

In sacred Scripture, numbers usually have more significance than just their quantitative indicators. Often, even when a number is used to indicate a certain quantity, the individual number given may point beyond the numerical value to a symbolic significance. At other times, the number given is not to be taken literally, and may represent an approximate value, a symbolic value, or it may indicate the use of hyperbole—an exaggeration or amplification to illustrate a teaching point in the Biblical text. For example, in the Holy Gospel according to St. Matthew, we read that Simon Peter asks Jesus how

---

8   Holy Bible: New Revised Standard Version. (1993). Catholic Bible Press.

many times he must forgive a brother who has sinned against him. Peter asks, "*As many as seven times?*" (Matthew 18:21). We read, "*Jesus said to him, 'Not seven times, but I tell you, seventy-seven times'*" (Matthew 18:22). Jesus's response indicates not a literal seventy-seven times, but that Peter's forgiveness is to be given without limit, an abundance of forgiveness. The "perfect" number seven represents fullness, covenant union, and spiritual perfection.

The Hebrews, Greeks, Romans, and many other ancient peoples used their alphabets for numbers. According to ancient tradition, each number has spiritual significance. The study of the significance of the use of numbers in scripture requires a lifetime of study and reflection, but a brief summary of some of the significant numbers may be enough to whet the reader's appetite for further investigation. Let's take a look at our earlier reference to the psalmist's description of the length of life as "*seventy years or perhaps eighty.*"

In sacred Scripture, the number seven represents spiritual perfection and fullness, or completion. It derives much of its meaning from being tied directly to God's creation of all things. Seven is the number of covenant and of the Holy Spirit. God rested on the seventh day after all the work He had done in Creation (Genesis 2:2); there are seven gifts of the Holy Spirit;[9] it took Solomon seven years to build the Temple in Jerusalem (1 Kings 6:38); the original sacred menorah had seven branches (six on each side of a central shaft) and seven cup-shaped lamps for the olive oil (Exodus 25:31).

The number seven is also significant in our natural world. To name a few, there are:

---

9   *Catechism of the Catholic Church* #1831.

- seven continents in the world: Africa, Asia, Antarctica, Australia/Oceania, Europe, North America, and South America

- seven days in the week

- seven notes in the musical scale

- seven colours in the spectrum (the seven-coloured rainbow being the sign of God's covenant with Noah)

- seven directions (left, right, up, down, forward, back, and centre)

In sacred Scripture, the number eight represents salvation, resurrection, and new birth/regeneration—a new beginning. It is the first of a new series: there are seven days in a week; the eighth day is the beginning of a new series of days. The eighth note on the musical scale introduces a new octave, a higher octave, much like the higher heavens to which we are ascending after the death of our mortal bodies. Eight is the first cubic number (2 x 2 x 2). This is significant because the Holy of Holies in the Tabernacle and in the Jerusalem Temple was the same height, length, and breadth—a perfect cube (1 Kings 6:20). David, God's anointed, was the eighth son of Jesse (1 Samuel 16:10–12). Eight people were saved in the ark during the Great Flood, including Noah, his wife, and his three sons and their wives (Genesis 7:13). In the natural world, scientists have identified eighty-eight constellations.[10] Scientists now believe there are only eight planets, given that Pluto's erratic orbit suggests it was once a moon of Neptune.

That brings us to the reason for my diversion into scriptural numerology—the length of life, described in sacred Scripture as "*seventy*

---

10   Constellation. (2021, October 5). In *Wikipedia*. en.wikipedia.org/wiki/Constellation

years or perhaps eighty." Taken together, the numbers seven and eight form a remarkable connection. And, the numbers seventy and eighty are multiples of their derivatives, seven and eight.

The number seven, therefore the number seventy (seven times ten) represents spiritual perfection and fullness, or completion. The number eight, therefore the number eighty (eight times ten) represents salvation, resurrection, and new birth/regeneration—a new beginning. In sacred Scripture, seventy years of life represent spiritual perfection and fullness, or completion, and eighty years of life speaks to a new birth/regeneration—a new beginning.

Unique among the psalms, Psalm 90 is attributed to having been written by Moses, toward the end of his years of wandering through the wilderness of the Sinai desert. This would make Psalm 90 the oldest in the Psalter. It is not surprising that the author speaks of a lifetime which is focused on reaching perfect completion and a prayer for new beginnings for the new generation of Israelites who were about to enter the Promised Land.

Moses's statement that humans live seventy to eighty years—a statement which was made more than 3,500 years ago—is surprisingly accurate today! Current data from the World Health Organization identifies that the life expectancy in the world for females is 81.2 years; for males, it's 76.4 years. In comparison, in Canada, the average life expectancy for those born in 2019 was 80 years for males and 84 years for females.

Chapter Two

Stereotypes: Are they Self-Fulfilling Prophecies?

Aging is a highly individualized and complex process, yet it continues to be stereotyped, especially in Western cultures. Stereotypes of aging in contemporary culture are primarily negative, depicting later life as a time of ill health, loneliness, dependency, and poor physical and mental functioning. However, stereotypes of aging can also be positive and include descriptors such as wise, kind, dependable, and trustworthy.

While these latter descriptors are honourable, it would be unrealistic to suggest that they are applicable to every older adult. Whenever an individual is presumed to be a certain way because of group membership, his or her individuality is at risk of being downplayed. Thus, even a positive stereotype has the tendency to reduce the older adult to a cliché instead of honouring their individuality.

Notably, any stereotype of aging (including those that equate aging with frailty and decline, or later life with health and affluence) has the potential to reinforce ageism, i.e., social oppression based on age. Stereotypes—positive or negative—fail to acknowledge the diversity among older adults and can be used to justify prejudice and discrimination.

11

In this chapter, we will look at how stereotypes about older adults can play a powerful role in shaping how we think about and interact with them, as well as how individuals within the group see themselves.[11] We will also look at some of the more common stereotypes which confront the older adult population.

Stereotypes of aging include assumptions and generalizations about how people at or over a certain age should behave, and what they are likely to experience, without regard for individual differences or unique circumstances.[12] Unfortunately, once we have developed a stereotype, we unconsciously seek to reinforce it and prove its truth. Rather than simply shaping perceptions (as if that is not bad enough in and of itself), the expectations that accompany the stereotype can create conditions which almost inevitably lead to their own confirmation. In other words, stereotypes can become self-fulfilling prophecies.

Let's begin with seeking a common understanding of stereotypes. A stereotype has been defined as an unchallenged myth or overstated belief—positive or negative—about the characteristics, attributes, or behaviours of members of a specific group that is applied generally to most members of the group. Stereotypes are often entrenched in verbal, written, and/or visual contexts within the society.[13] They are generally negative, and have little or no connection to the actual behaviour of individual members of the groups being stereotyped.

---

11   Horton, S., Baker, J. and Deakin, J.M. (2007). Stereotypes of aging: their effects on the health of seniors in North American society. *Educational Gerontology, vol. 33*, no. 12, pp. 1021–1035.

12   Ory, M., Hoffman, M.K., Hawkins, M., Sanner, B. and Mockenhaupt, R. (2003). Challenging aging stereotypes: strategies for creating a more active society. *American Journal of Preventive Medicine, vol. 25*, supplement 2, no. 3, pp. 164–171.

13   Allport, G.W. (1958). *The nature of prejudice*. Addison-Wesley.

As one example, Snyder et al.[14] examined the self-fulfilling influences of social stereotypes on social interaction, a study in which undergraduate men and women participated in an experiment about first encounters. Subjects were told that the experiment involved a telephone conversation with a stranger of the opposite gender. The men, but not the women, then had their pictures taken with an instant camera and were given pictures of the women who were allegedly their conversational partners.

In actual fact, the pictures the men received were not ones of their conversation partners. Instead, half of the men received a picture of a physically attractive woman, and the other received a picture of a woman who was not physically attractive. The subjects held brief telephone conversations, which were recorded, and then provided their general impressions of their conversation partners.

The men who thought they were talking with an attractive woman rated their partners more positively than did those men who thought otherwise. But what is even more noteworthy is that the attractiveness stereotypes changed the behaviour of the women who were conversation partners. When judges later listened to the conversations, they found that the women (who had spoken with a man shown the picture of an attractive woman) behaved in more likeable, sociable, and animated ways than those women who spoke with a man who had been shown the picture of an unattractive woman. The men's stereotype-based expectations that beautiful women do beautiful things became true. Women who were the target of the beautiful stereotype came to behave more "beautifully" in the conversations.

---

14 Snyder, M., Tanke, E., and Decker, Berscheid, Ellen. (1977). Social perception and interpersonal behaviour: On the self-fulfilling nature of social stereotypes. *Journal of Personality and Social Psychology, 35*(9), 656–666.

How did this happen? It appears to have been because the men who thought they were talking with an attractive woman invested more in the conversation than the men who thought they were talking with an unattractive woman. As a result, they behaved more sociably. And, their partners responded in kind.

Let's look at another example, this time related specifically to older adults. Research on aging and memory has produced an impressive body of work demonstrating that memory abilities decline with age[15]. Many have suggested that this decline is associated with physiological changes, including sensory and other neural deficits,[16] while a parallel body of research has examined the role that people's beliefs about their memory ability play into their performance.[17]

Chasteen et al.[18] showed that age differences in memory performance were mediated by participants' feelings of stereotype threat, such that age was positively related to stereotype threat (i.e., the older the adult, the greater the influence of the threat of being stereotyped), and stereotype threat was negatively related to memory performance (i.e., the greater the threat of being stereotyped, the poorer the performance). This data demonstrates that, for older adults,

---

15   Zacks, R. T., Hasher L., & Li, K. Z. H. (2000). Human memory. In: Craik, F. I M., & Salthouse, T. A. (Eds.). *The handbook of aging and cognition* (2nd ed.). Lawrence Erlbaum Associates Publishers. pp. 293–358.

16   Schneider, B. A., & Pichora-Fuller, M. K. (2000). Implications of perceptual deterioration for cognitive aging research. In: Craik, F. I. M., & Salthouse, T. A. (Eds). *The handbook of aging and cognition* (2nd ed.). Lawrence Erlbaum Associates Publishers. pp. 155–220.

17   Hertzog ,C., & Hultsch, D. (2000). Metacognition in adulthood and old age. In: Craik, F. I. M., & Salthouse, T. A. (Eds.). *The handbook of aging and cognition* (2nd ed.). Lawrence Erlbaum Associates Publishers. pp. 417–466.

18   Chasteen, A., Bhattacharyya, S., Horhota, M., Tam, R., & Hasher, L. (2005). How feelings of stereotype threat influence older adults' memory performance. *Experimental Aging Research, 31*(3), 235–260.

being negatively stereotyped influences memory performance, and the effects of these feelings on performance are not easily reduced by reframing the task instructions.

In short, stereotypes can create self-fulfilling prophecies. We tend to do, and attempt to be, that which our immediate cohort of influence expects us to do and to be. And therein lies the insidious danger of demographic stereotypes. Over time, they become self-fulfilling. When a message purporting to define who and what we are is repeated often enough, we tend to internalize and come to believe the message. Whether or not it is true becomes irrelevant.

In conclusion, stereotypes can be dangerous. They not only shape our attitude toward a group of people, but they also shape the behaviour of that group. If we are a part of that group, our own attitudes and expectations can be adversely affected by society's stereotypes of us. In other words, with our stereotype lenses, we will see what we want to see. What we expect is what we will get.[19]

So, with that as a backdrop, let's look at some of our society's stereotypical beliefs about older adults.

---

19   Ramona Big Eagle Moore. (2016). *Story about elephant.* Native American Culture and Racial Identity Lecture. John Lewis Fellowship.

Stereotyped Belief	Reality
Positive Stereotypes	
Older adults are wise	Research findings suggest that older people are more likely to behave in rational ways and they tend to be more emotionally stable,[20] both of which may be indicators of wisdom. That being said, wisdom is not easy to measure. By virtue of their advanced years, older adults have the benefit of more life experiences. Does that necessarily make someone wise? Wisdom comes from the lessons learned from our life experiences, not from merely surviving those experiences. Hence, while some older adults are likely wise, others may not be.
Older adults are kind	Research indicates that people tend to become more agreeable, more conscientious, and less neurotic as they age.[21] Perhaps this translates as "kind," but there are other factors which likely influence kindness, factors such as current mood state, presence or absence of physical pain or discomfort, current problems being faced, and personality traits.
Older adults are dependable	Older adults may be more dependable when compared to their more youthful counterparts, and research supports this to some degree. For example, older adults have the lowest crime rates among all age groups, and in a work setting, they have lower absenteeism and turnover rates.[22] But, these facts do not reflect those older adults who are generally unreliable in other ways, including those who commit crimes, miss a significant number of workdays, and misuse drugs.

---

20   North, M. S., & Fiske, S. T. (2012). An inconvenienced youth? Ageism and its potential intergenerational roots. *Psychological Bulletin*. American Psychological Association.

21   Allemand, M., Zimprich, D., & Hertzog, C. (2007). *Cross-sectional age differences and longitudinal age changes of personality in middle adulthood and old age.* PubMed.gov. U.S. Library of Medicine.

22   Palmore, E. B. (1998). *The facts on aging quiz.* Springer.

Older adults are happy or serene	Older adults may be somewhat happier than their younger counterparts. Based on research, it appears that negative emotions decline with age, while positive emotions remain fairly stable throughout middle age, with only a slight decrease in older adulthood.[23] Depression is less common in older adulthood, while reported life satisfaction tends to be relatively stable across different life stages.[24] So, while older adults may be better at regulating their emotions and they may experience a decrease in negative emotions as they age, the extent to which an older adult is happy or serene will be shaped by such personal factors as personality, previous levels of happiness, life satisfaction, current stress levels, and access to resources.
Negative Stereotypes	
Older adults are sickly and disabled	While the vast majority of older adults have one or more chronic conditions such as hypertension or high cholesterol, so do many middle-age adults.[25] This doesn't necessarily mean that all older individuals have drastically worse health than their younger counterparts. Most of these conditions are manageable with the help of a medical practitioner. Many individuals live active, healthy lives well into their 80s and 90s. According to Statistics Canada, for those over 65 years of age, 44% rated their health as excellent or very good as compared to 64% of those aged 18 to 64 years of age.[26]

23 Charles, S. T., Reynolds, C. A., & Gatz, M. (2001). Age-related differences and change in positive and negative affect over 23 years. *Journal of Personality and Social Psychology*. Vol. 80, No. 1, 136–151.

24 Diener, E., & Suh, M. E. (1998). Subjective well-being and age: An international analysis. *Annual Review of Gerontology and Geriatrics: Focus on Emotion and Adult Development*. Springer.

25 Government of Canada. (2019). *Chronic disease data and indicators*. https://www.canada.ca/en/public-health/services/chronic-diseases/chronic-disease-facts-figures.html

26 Government of Canada. (2019). *Chronic disease data and indicators*. https://www.canada.ca/en/public-health/services/chronic-diseases/chronic-disease-facts-figures.html

Aging leads to loss of teeth	Good oral care and regular checkups play an important role in maintaining good oral health among seniors. Canadians' oral health is comparable to, or better than, the oral health of citizens in most developed countries. According to a Canadian Health Measures Survey, approximately 20% of Canadians aged 60 to 79 are without teeth or edentulous. Even in the oldest age group, 75 and older, only about one in four individuals (or 25%) have lost all their teeth. Approximately 32% of Canadians have no dental insurance, and many people avoid visiting a dental professional due to concerns about cost.[27]
Aging leads to memory loss	"Senior moments" are not normal. Let's face it, individuals of all ages are likely to misplace their keys or forget things from time to time. And, while some change in thinking patterns is a normal part of the aging process, memory loss is not. Sometimes difficulty with memory may be due to related medical conditions, and sometimes it may be related to dementia. No matter what the cause, if you or a loved one is experiencing a noticeable change in memory, it is important to talk to your doctor about it. Memory loss should never be attributed as simply a "normal part of aging."
Aging leads to neurocognitive impairment, e.g., dementia	The Alzheimer's Society of Canada identifies that neurocognitive impairment is not part of the normal aging process, and many older adults do not have significant impairment in memory or functioning.[28] While Alzheimer's disease is the most prevalent type of cognitive impairment, current thinking suggests that healthy lifestyle choices such as remaining active and adding aerobic exercise several times each week improves information processing in older adults.[29] Studies such as these indicate the plasticity of cognition and the fact that its loss is not a normal part of the aging process.[30]

27   Statistics Canada. (2009). *Canadian Health Measures Survey*. Ottawa.

28   Alzheimer's Society of Canada. (2012).

29   Staudinger, U. M. (2015). Images of aging: outside and inside perspectives. *Annual Review of Gerontology and Geriatrics 35*, 187–210.

30   Alzheimer's Society of Canada. (2020). https://alzheimer.ca/en/Home/About-dementia/Brain-health

	Around 30–40% of adults over 65 have the type of cognitive loss we regard as a normal consequence of age, which is a measurable (but slight) decline on memory tests—a feeling that you're not quite as sharp or as good at remembering as you used to be. Around 10% of adults over 65 develop mild cognitive impairment, which does impact everyday living, and is a precursor to Alzheimer's. It is estimated that more than 432,000 Canadians over the age of 65 were living with diagnosed dementia in Canada in 2016–17, two thirds of whom were women.[31] Age is an important risk factor for dementia, and as Canada's population ages, the number of Canadians living with dementia is expected to rise. Nine seniors are diagnosed with dementia every hour, and the risk of being diagnosed with dementia doubles with every five-year increase in age between the ages of 65 and 84. Statistics show that 0.8% of Canadians aged 65 to 69 years are diagnosed with dementia, compared to 31.5% of those aged 90 years and older.[32] While most people with dementia are over the age of 65, a small number of people in their 40s and 50s can, and do, develop dementia-related diseases.[33]
The pain and disability caused by arthritis is inevitable as you get older	While arthritis is more common as we age, thanks to the impact of time on the cushiony cartilage that prevents joints and bone from rubbing against one another, age itself doesn't cause arthritis. The American College of Rheumatology[34] identifies that steps can be taken to prevent arthritis or reduce its impact, including losing weight, wearing comfortable, supportive shoes, and taking it easy with joint-debilitating exercise such as running and basketball. One study found that women who exercised at least once every two weeks for at least 20 minutes were much less likely to develop arthritis of the knee (the most common location for the disease) than women who exercised less.

31   Statistics Canada. (2019). *A Dementia Strategy for Canada: Together We Aspire.* Ottawa.

32   Statistics Canada. (2019). *A Dementia Strategy for Canada: Together We Aspire.* Ottawa.

33   Statistics Canada. (2019). *A Dementia Strategy for Canada: Together We Aspire.* Ottawa.

34   The American College of Rheumatology Communications and Marketing Committee. (December 2020). *Exercise and arthritis.* Rheumatology.org. https://www.rheumatology.org/I-Am-A/Patient-Caregiver/Diseases-Conditions/Living-Well-with-Rheumatic-Disease/Exercise-and-Arthritis

Aging inevitably leads to living in a long-term care facility	Over half of all older adults not living in a care facility are living with their spouse, and about 28% live alone.[35] Due to their increased longevity, women are more likely to live alone. Most individuals want to "age in place" in their current home. The good news is that most people are able to do so. Of the almost 5 million seniors age 65 and older in Canada, 7.1% live in care facilities—nursing homes, chronic care, or long-term care hospitals (4.5%), or residences for seniors (2.6%). Census data from 2016 also show that although most seniors are living in their own homes, one third (32%) of seniors age 85 and over live in collective dwellings, such as nursing homes and residences for senior citizens.[36]
Older adults cannot change and are stubborn	Older adults have the capacity to continue to learn new things as they age, and research indicates that older adults respond well to therapeutic interventions.[37] Being open to change and having the opportunity to explore new and novel situations, ideas, and activities are important factors when considering the ability (and desire) to change. In fact, evidence suggests that when older adults are exposed to new activities, their openness to novel experiences increases.[38]
Older adults are unproductive or a burden on society	Another common misconception is the idea that older adults are slower, less productive employees. However, older adults tend to have a significant organizational success work ethic. Irrespective of the generation of worker, be it traditionalist, baby boomer, Gen X, millennial, or Generation Z, each have their own distinct motivators in the workforce. Beyond work ethic, older individuals are likely to bring years of experience with them.

35 US Department of Health and Human Services. (2013).

36 Statistics Canada. (2017). *2016 census of population: Families, households, marital status, structural type of dwelling, collectives.* Ottawa.

37 Stanley, M. A. et al. (2009). Cognitive behaviour therapy for generalized anxiety disorder among older adults in primary care: A randomized clinical trial. *JAMA*, 301, 1460–1467.

38 Staudinger, U. M. (2015). Images of aging: outside and inside perspectives. *Annual Review of Gerontology and Geriatrics*, 35, 187–210.

In 2015, one in five Canadians aged 65 and older, or nearly 1.1 million seniors, reported working during the year. This is the highest proportion recorded since the 1981 census.[39]

Productivity is not simply measured by paid work. Volunteering is a significant contributor to our country's gross national product (GNP). Volunteering is generally defined as unpaid work for or through an organization. It is distinct from informal helping or caregiving, in which people may assist neighbours or friends with certain tasks, such as grocery shopping, childcare, or yard work.

According to the 2010 Canada Survey of Giving, Volunteering, and Participating,[40] seniors (adults over the age of 65) volunteered an average of 223 hours per year, higher than any other age group.

The volunteer rate (36.5%) for seniors is lower than the rate for all Canadians (47%) over the age of 15. Comparing three specific age groups, shadow boomers (45–54 years of age), baby boomers (55–64 years of age), and seniors (65 years of age and older) indicates that the volunteer rate decreases with age, while the average number of hours increases with age. However, by separating younger seniors (65–74) and older seniors (75+), there is a distinction evident with 40% of younger seniors volunteering an average of 235 hours each year, while 31% of older seniors volunteer an average of 198 hours each year. This is likely explained by the limitations that may be created from the health and mobility issues that increase with age, while availability tends to increase with age due to fewer work and family responsibilities.

Older people tend to devote many more hours to volunteer activities than middle-aged and younger adults. In addition, grandparents are primary caregivers for approximately 6% of children under the age of 18 years.[41]

---

39   Statistics Canada. (2017). *Working seniors in Canada*. Ottawa.
40   Volunteer Canada. (2013). *Volunteering and older adults: Final report.* https://volunteer.ca/vdemo/EngagingVolunteers_DOCS/Volunteering_and_Older_Adults_Final_Report_2013.pdf.
41   US Census Bureau. (2014).

Older adults are lonely and isolated	The 2011 Census of Population reported that 92.1% of older adults lived in private households or dwellings (as part of couples, alone, or with others), while 7.9% lived in collective dwellings, such as residences for senior citizens or health-care and related facilities. These proportions were relatively unchanged from 2001 when 92.6% of the senior population lived in private households and 7.4% lived in collective dwellings.[42] Most older adults lived as a couple with either a married spouse or a common-law partner during their early senior years. The size of the population of older seniors was smaller, owing to higher mortality rates. At the oldest ages, fewer people lived in private households, specifically in couples, and comparatively more lived in collective dwellings. In a longitudinal study, older adults who had a previous high level of social engagement decreased their involvement only slightly over time.[43] Thus, one's level of social involvement earlier in life is likely mirrored in later life. Moreover, the replacement of friends is a dynamic process that does not change much with advancing years. In other words, new friendships tend to replace old friendships as people move away, lose touch, or die.
Depression is common among older adults	Depression is less prevalent in older adults than their younger counterparts.[44] However, when it occurs, it can be particularly detrimental for older adults. Older adults who are depressed are more likely to develop memory and learning problems, and depression has been linked to an increased risk of death from numerous age-related diseases, including Parkinson's disease, stroke, and pneumonia. Growing older can involve significant life changes, including retirement, the death of loved ones, and increased medical problems. It is normal to feel sad or uneasy about these changes. However, depression is not a normal part of aging. Rather, it is a medical condition that interferes with normal functioning.

42 Statistics Canada. (2013). *Living arrangements of seniors*. Ottawa. https://www12. statcan.gc.ca/census-recensement/2011/as-sa/98-312-x/98-312-x2011003_4-eng.cfm

43 Thomas, M. (2011). Villages: Helping people age in place. *AARP The Magazine*. May/ June 2011.

44 Fiske, A., Wetherell, J. L., & Gatz, M. (2009). Depression in older adults. *Annual Review of Clinical Psychology*, 5, 363–389.

Older adults are poor	The overwhelming percentage of older adults are financially self-sufficient. However, evidence demonstrates that single, unattached older adults, as well as older women, remain the most financially vulnerable members of our society. According to the low-income measure after tax (LIM-AT), 6.2% of attached older adults as compared to 28.5% of single older adults in Canada are considered low-income.[45] Additionally, older Canadian women *"are twice as likely to live in poverty as men,"* with 30% of older Canadian women living below the poverty line.[46] This striking difference can be explained largely due to a greater likelihood of gaps in their workforce participation, while at the same time experiencing longer life expectancies. Due to prior workforce participation gaps, older Canadian women are far more reliant on publicly funded federal income supports such as federal old age security (OAS) and guaranteed income supplement (GIS) versus contribution-dependent pension plans such as the Canada Pension Plan (CPP), the Quebec Pension Plan (QPP), and private pension schemes. In fact, 30% of an older Canadian woman's total income is supported by OAS and GIS, compared to 18% of their male counterparts.[47] Though supports such as GIS do take into account marital status in an effort to recognize gender inequity in retirement income, the fact that 30% of older Canadian women still live below the poverty line demonstrates that marital status considerations do not adequately offset the gender gap. Inequity of this scale, therefore, remains a cause for great concern and should be addressed in future income support funding reforms.

45   Statistics Canada. (2014). Canadian income survey, 2012. *Statistics Canada Catalogue*, no. 11-001-X. http://www.statcan.gc.ca/daily-quotidien/141210/dq141210a-eng.pdf

46   http://www.policyschool.ucalgary.ca/sites/default/files/research/mintz-bazel-seniors-income.pdf

47   http://canadianlabour.ca/issues-research/did-you-know-senior-women-are-twice-likely-live-poverty-men

Older adults are sexually inactive/ not interested in sex	In a recent study, 18% of men and 8% of women aged 60 to 69 reported having sexual intercourse once or twice a month, and 45% and 35% respectively reported daily kissing and hugging. Additionally, 11% of both men and women in this same age group report self-stimulation once or twice per month.[48] Attitudes toward sexual expression shape behaviour, and, as baby boomers reach older age, additional shifts in sexual activity will likely occur, given the generation in which they were raised.
Older adults are grouchy and grumpy	The ability to regulate emotions improves with age,[49] and thus there is no reason to believe that older adults are grumpier than any other age group. In one study, it was reported that neutral facial expressions were often misread as sad by younger people.[50] So, perhaps there is a misinterpretation of mood based on misread affect. Also, if someone is in physical pain, e.g., arthritis, or is feeling frustrated or overwhelmed, such as might occur in a fast-moving society, the individual may be on edge, but this can happen irrespective of the person's chronological age.
Older adults cannot use technology or learn new things	While older adults have tended to be late adopters of technology, a recent study reported that 60% of older adults use the internet and of those individuals, 71% go online every day or almost every day. Also, 77% of older adults have a cellphone. Income and access to electronic devices play a role in the use of technology, as do physical challenges.[51]
Older adults are bad drivers	We've all seen older drivers portrayed in the media as the little old lady hunched behind the steering wheel, driving well below the speed limit. The reality is that older adults are not all bad drivers. In fact, compared to younger individuals, older adults have fewer crashes per mile driven. They are less likely to drive while intoxicated or texting. They are also more likely to self-regulate or restrict driving during bad weather, at night, and on unfamiliar roads.

48   Fisher, Linda. (2010). Sex, romance, and relationships: AARP survey of midlife and older adults. *AARP Research.* https://www.aarp.org/research/topics/life/info-2014/srr_09.html.

49   Carstensen, L. L., & Mikels, J. A. (2005). At the intersection of emotion and cognition: Aging and the positivity effect. *Current directions in psychological science,* 14, 117–121.

50   Fölster, M., Hess, U., and Werheid, K. (2014). Facial age affects emotional expression decoding. Frontiers in Psychology. https://doi.org/10.3389/fpsyg.2014.00030.

51   Pew Research Centre. (2014). Attitudes about aging: A global perspective.

	Unfortunately, when involved in a crash, older individuals are more likely to suffer fatal injuries. However, this is likely tied to age-associated health conditions. In a 2011 report by the Government of Canada, drivers aged 65 and over represented 17% of the fatalities, even though they only accounted for 14% of the licensed drivers. In the report, the rate of fatalities per distance travelled started to increase considerably at 75 years of age and over. Part of the reason for this greater risk of fatality is that seniors are more fragile, and if they are involved in a collision, they are more likely to be seriously injured or killed. As seniors age, they are more likely to develop physical and cognitive infirmities, although not all seniors have conditions which affect the safety of their driving. Hence, age should not be used as the basis for determining whether a driver can continue to drive. Rather, such a decision should be based on the driver's physical and cognitive fitness to drive safely. A balance has to be maintained between the mobility of seniors and road safety.[52]
Falls are a normal part of aging	While it is true that many older individuals will experience a fall, this is certainly not a normal or inevitable part of aging. Falls are dangerous and should never be dismissed as "normal." Evidence shows that many falls can be prevented through medication adjustments, having your vision checked, strength and balance exercises, and keeping your home free of tripping hazards.

We wrap up this chapter knowing that stereotypes can be dangerous. Judging any group by a set of primarily negative characteristics ignores both the breadth of human experience evident in any group of people, and the unique individuality of each member of the group. When those pre-judgements are used to generalize groups of people, as human creatures we tend to emphasize how we are different from the group. By focusing on differences, often by accentuating negative traits, we build stereotypes by defining ourselves as separate from others.

---

52   Government of Canada. (2011). *Road safety in Canada.* https://www.tc.gc.ca/media/documents/roadsafety/tp15145e.pdf

However, when we apply the same process of differentiation to individuals we meet in daily life, we tend to emphasize positive traits, looking not for how the individual is different from ourselves, but how he or she is the same. By emphasizing commonalities, we break down stereotypes.

The takeaway, my friends, is that you are called to be aware of the power of stereotyping groups—in this case, older adults. If you are a younger person, then I encourage you, when interacting with older adults that you be conscious of our society's stereotypes and that you make every attempt to avoid pigeonholing that person or that group and thereby limiting their potential contribution. Look beyond the stereotypes and interact fully with the individual in front of you.

If you are an older adult, I encourage you to refuse to be limited by society's stereotypes about your demographic. Refuse to accept those stereotypes as descriptive of all that you are and all that you aspire to be. Be all that you can be for every moment that you can be it.

If you are looking for undeniable proof that it's never too late and you're never too old, look no further than Jenny Joseph's poem titled "*Warning.*" A 1996 survey by the British Broadcasting Corporation identified this poem as the United Kingdom's most popular post-war poetry related to aging, beating Dylan Thomas's "*Do Not Go Gentle Into That Good Night.*" The poem goes like this:

> *When I am an old woman I shall wear purple*
> *With a red hat which doesn't go, and doesn't suit me.*
> *And I shall spend my pension on brandy and summer gloves*
> *And satin sandals, and say we've no money for butter.*
> *I shall sit down on the pavement when I'm tired*

And gobble up samples in shops and press alarm bells
And run my stick along the public railings
And make up for the sobriety of my youth.
I shall go out in my slippers in the rain
And pick the flowers in other people's gardens
And learn to spit.

You can wear terrible shirts and grow more fat
And eat three pounds of sausages at a go
Or only bread and pickle for a week
And hoard pens and pencils and beermats and things in boxes.

But now we must have clothes that keep us dry
And pay our rent and not swear in the street
And set a good example for the children.
We must have friends to dinner and read the papers.

But maybe I ought to practise a little now?
So people who know me are not too shocked and surprised
When suddenly I am old, and start to wear purple.[53]

And, since I referenced him above, the Welsh poet Dylan Thomas[54]
says it this way in his immortal words:

Do not go gentle into that good night,
Old age should burn and rave at close of day;
Rage, rage against the dying of the light.

---

53   Joseph, Jenny. (1992). *Selected Poems*. Bloodaxe Books.
54   Thomas, Dylan. (1914–1953). *Do not go gentle into that good night*. https://poets.org/
poem/do-not-go-gentle-good-night.

Though wise men at their end know dark is right,
Because their words had forked no lightning they
Do not go gentle into that good night.

Good men, the last wave by, crying how bright
Their frail deeds might have danced in a green bay,
Rage, rage against the dying of the light.

Wild men who caught and sang the sun in flight,
And learn, too late, they grieved it on its way,
Do not go gentle into that good night.

Grave men, near death, who see with blinding sight
Blind eyes could blaze like meteors and be gay,
Rage, rage against the dying of the light.

And you, my father, there on the sad height,
Curse, bless, me now with your fierce tears, I pray.
Do not go gentle into that good night.
Rage, rage against the dying of the light.

Although Thomas's poem offers a defiant attitude toward death, rather than the usual "passed away peacefully," which one reads in the obituary columns of newspapers, I believe that his poem speaks equally to the aging process and life as lived out by older adults. It is a poem which affirms life.

My friends, do not go gentle into that good night. Old age should burn and rave at close of day. Rage, rage against the dying of the light.

In closing, I encourage you to take a brief quiz to determine your knowledge on a few other myths not addressed in the previous pages. Answer **true** or **false** to each statement.

1. Polypharmacy (administration of many drugs together) can lead to a change in mental status.

2. Aging is a universal phenomenon.

3. Older adults may present with atypical symptoms that complicate diagnosis.

4. The body's reaction to changes in medications remains constant with advancing age.

5. If one observes a sudden change in mental status in an older adult, medication side effects should be investigated as a likely cause.

6. Primary causes of delirium in older adults include medications, dehydration, and infection.

7. Dehydration is not common in older adults.

8. Older adults experiencing a decline in daily function will show no benefit from early rehabilitation.

9. A decline in functional ability for a person residing in a long-term care facility may indicate the onset of a new illness.

10. Urinary incontinence is so common in older adults that it could be considered a normal part of aging.

Answers can be found on the next page. No peeking before you finish the quiz!

Quiz Answer Key:

1. Polypharmacy (administration of many drugs together) can lead to a change in mental status. **True**

2. Aging is a universal phenomenon. **True**

3. Older adults may present with atypical symptoms that complicate diagnosis. **True**

4. The body's reaction to changes in medications remains constant with advancing age. **False**

5. If one observes a sudden change in mental status in an older adult, medication side effects should be investigated as a likely cause. **True**

6. Primary causes of delirium in older adults include medications, dehydration, and infection. **True**

7. Dehydration is not common in older adults. **False**

8. Older adults experiencing a decline in daily function will show no benefit from early rehabilitation. **False**

9. A decline in functional ability for a person residing in a long-term care facility may indicate the onset of a new illness. **True**

10. Urinary incontinence is so common in older adults that it could be considered a normal part of aging. **False**

Chapter Three

God Does Not Look Away

My cancer experience over the past nine years has been an unend-ing series of ups and downs. As it turned out, my cancer had not metastasized. Rather, it consisted of two separate sets of malignant cells growing completely independent of one another. One set of cells was growing in my bladder wall, the other in my prostate. Was it by accident or by God's design that my cancers were discovered as early as they were?

How was it found? An elevated PSA[55] of 5.8 at a routine medical, a digital exam, and me telling my family physician that I had a history of bladder infections. I've had a lot of kidney infections over the years, but not bladder infections. Why did I tell my doctor that I had recurrent bladder infections? I would come to understand that was God prompting my words. You see, in my case, this statement led to my family physician ordering an ultrasound of my bladder, which

---

55   A prostate-specific antigen (PSA) test measures the amount of PSA in the blood. PSA
     is a protein made by prostate cells. A PSA test may be done to help find prostate cancer
     early in men who don't have any signs or symptoms of the disease, to confirm a
     diagnosis of prostate cancer, to plan treatment, to find out if cancer treatments are
     working, and to find out if cancer has recurred after treatment.

revealed a tumour growing in the bladder wall. Because of that ultrasound, the tumour was discovered early. It was superficial, and was successfully removed surgically before it could invade the deeper tissues and break open to spread further into my urinary tract.

The Canadian Cancer Society recommends that men 50 years and older should talk to their doctor about their personal risk of developing prostate cancer, and discuss the benefits and risks of having a PSA test. Now, listen up, men, the Canadian Cancer Society also recommends that you talk to your doctor about PSA testing before age 50 if you:

- have a family history of prostate cancer or are of African ancestry
- have symptoms of prostate cancer

I am living testimony that a PSA test can detect prostate cancer early, before the tumour is large or spreads outside of the prostate. Finding cancer early can mean that treatments will be more successful. In my case, my drastically elevated PSA prompted a referral to a urologic oncologist—the one who told me on a cold winter afternoon in February 2011 that my cancer had metastasized.

My medical treatment consisted of two separate surgeries. One to remove the growth on my bladder wall, and a year later, another to remove the prostate tumour. In those first few days following the telephone call with my dispassionate—or should I say indifferent—surgeon-to-be, still in shock, I made a phone call to the Cancer Centres of America. Why? Because my son, Nathan, did what the surgeon had advised. He went to the public library and took out a few books on prostate cancer, and then brought them home for me to read. I read about the Cancer Centres of America, and I learned that they were world leaders in cancer treatment and cancer care. So, I phoned to speak with one of the Centre's staff.

I was advised to find two health professionals in my home community: a competent acupuncturist and a live cell analyst/nutritionist.[56] Over time, I came to realize that both of these professionals, together with my family physician, were concerned with treating me holistically.[57] To my urologic oncologist, I seemed to be not much more than a human carcass to be poked and prodded. To my family physician, my acupuncturist, and my nutritionist, I was more than my disease. I was a person … one who was on an emotional and spiritual roller coaster; someone who had feelings, concerns, fears, and doubts; a person who desperately wanted to be healthy once again.

These three health professionals did not work at cross-purposes with my surgeon, they just dealt with other equally critical aspects of my disease and my recovery—aspects of my health in which the surgeon had no apparent interest. The surgeon removed the tumours from my body and he walked away. My family physician, acupuncturist, and nutritionist journeyed with me to health, and they continue to do so to this day.

Now, don't misunderstand me. My intent is not to denigrate my urologic oncologist. In a post-surgical hospital follow-up, one of the

---

56 Live and Dry Blood Cell Analysis is used in observing and monitoring the state and/ or dysfunction of the body's systems and organs. The largest advantage is its ability to pick up health problems in their earliest stages, identifying toxicities and deficiencies in the immune system, and suggesting a holistic plan including elements of supplementation, diet, exercise, and other therapies.

57 The concept of holistic health embodies the understanding that the physical, mental, social, and spiritual aspects of a person's life must be viewed as an integrated whole; and the complete person, physically and psychologically, must be considered in the treatment of a disease.

nurses suggested that I might want to have a conversation with my family physician about a referral to a different specialist.

As I would later come to realize, that nurse's advice came from a higher prompting. As a result, I was referred to another urology specialist. This urologic oncologist has a caring bedside manner, provides the annual checkups in a positive and respectful manner, and is always approachable and informative. I am happy to announce that, earlier this year, I received good news of health at my ninth annual checkup—one more annual check-up to go before I am declared to be cancer free.

The take-away from all of this is that I want you to know that you can have victory in your life despite the struggles that you face. You can have victory in your life when you come to understand that God is working all things for your good and for His purpose for your life.

In sacred Scripture, we read:

> *We know that all things work together for good for those who love God, who are called according to his purpose. For those whom he foreknew he also predestined to be conformed to the image of his Son, in order that he might be the firstborn within a large family. And those whom he predestined he also called; and those whom he called he also justified; and those whom he justified he also glorified* (Romans 8:28–30).[58]

My friends, all things work together for good for those who love God. Even though your whole world may seem like it's falling apart, it is actually falling into place. God is going to use the seemingly

---

58   Holy Bible: New Revised Standard Version. (1993). Catholic Bible Press.

insurmountable obstacles in your path for your good and for His glory.

So many times, we feel that God is unaware of, or unconcerned with, our painful trials. But nothing could be further from the truth. Father God has a divine, eternal reason for each and every thing that you endure. He has a timing for it all, and, if you can trust in Him and in His infinite mercy, it is all part of His perfect plan.

Understandably, it is easier to trust God when things are going well. How much more difficult it is to believe in God's grace when we are faced on every side by personal turmoil. When we encounter seemingly unending difficulty, we may think that God has disappeared or that He is displeased with us. To whom can you turn when your eyes cannot cry another tear? What consoles you when there are no other medical options? How can you be comforted when relationships are shattered? To whom can you turn when many falsely accuse you? How can you be strengthened to stand when tragedy has buckled your knees?

I once read that no matter how deep the pit that we are in, God is with us. We can never sink lower than Christ can descend. We can never outrun His loving sovereignty. He joins us in the pit to give us more of Himself. God is with you in the pit for His glory and your good. He will never abandon you.

We look in the Old Testament to the trials of Job. Job was a wealthy man with a wife, children, and servants. He honoured God with all he had and held nothing back from Him. We read that, *"There was once a man in the land of Uz whose name was Job. That man was blameless and upright, one who feared God and turned away from evil*" (Job 1:1). Yet God allowed Satan to attack Job and take his children, his wealth, his servants, and even his health. Job was reduced to a painful existence living outside of his home because he was deemed unclean due to the infestation of boils that was afflicting his whole body. His own wife told him to "*Curse your God and die*" (Job 2:9). What did Job say to her remark? He answered, "*You speak as any foolish woman would speak. Shall we receive the good at the hand of God, and not receive the bad?*" (Job 2:10).

That is a question we all need to ask ourselves. Is it okay with us to take the good from God, and then turn away from Him in times of trouble? Does God owe us anything? It is by His grace, by His unmerited favour, that we receive all the good that we have. We are in His hands, and He alone knows how to get us from where we are to where He is, to our heavenly home.

My friends, know with absolute certainty—know with every ounce of your being—that Father God does not look away from you for a second. We always have hope, even and especially in the midst of the darkest storms, for Christ lives to intercede for us. We read in Psalm 91 that:

> *You who live in the shelter of the Most High, who abide in the shadow of the Almighty, will say to the Lord, "My refuge and my fortress; my God, in whom I trust." For he will deliver you from the snare of the fowler and from the deadly pestilence; he will cover you with his pinions, and under his wings you will find refuge; his faithfulness is a shield and buckler.*

You will not fear the terror of the night, nor the arrow that flies by day, nor the pestilence that stalks in darkness, nor the destruction that wastes at noonday. A thousand may fall at your side, ten thousand at your right hand, but it will not come near you.

Because you have made the Lord your refuge, the Most High your dwelling place, no evil shall befall you, no scourge come near your tent.

For he will command his angels concerning you to guard you in all your ways. On their hands they will bear you up, so that you will not dash your foot against a stone. You will tread on the lion and the adder, the young lion and the serpent you will trample under foot.

Those who love me, I will deliver; I will protect those who know my name. When they call to me, I will answer them; I will be with them in trouble, I will rescue them and honor them. With long life I will satisfy them, and show them my salvation.

He commands His angels to guard our path and guide our steps. We are not left to fend for ourselves when darkness comes. With Christ, we have all the hope and peace needed to get through the pain as God works through it to reveal more of Himself to us. No battle is too big for Him, because he has authority over everything. The outcome is always in His hands.

Whatever you are going through, stay focused on the fact that God has created a way to help you. God gives and God allows things to be taken, but it all is part of the plan to give you eternal life in a kingdom that will have no end. And because of that promise, we can praise God in every situation.

My friends, remember that we serve a loving God who can do far beyond what we mere mortals may think or even imagine to be possible. In the midst of your turmoil, like my cold Friday post-telephone call despair, just breathe. You may not be able to see a way forward right now. In fact, right now, there may not be a way forward. But, while your anxiety is temporary, know that the Lord and His outpouring grace are everlasting. While you are in the depth of your despair, God is moving in ways you don't understand, in ways that you can't even imagine. Be still and allow Him to calm the storm in your heart.

My favourite Celtic artist, Robin Mark,[59] sings it this way:

> *Blessed be Your name in the land that is plentiful*
> *Where Your streams of abundance flow*
> *Blessed be Your name*
>
> *And Blessed be Your name when I'm found in the desert place*
> *Though I walk through the wilderness*
> *Blessed be Your name*
>
> *Every blessing You pour out*
> *I'll turn back to praise*
> *And when the darkness closes in, Lord*
> *Still I will say*
> *Blessed be Your name*

---

59   Condensed from https://genius.com/Robin-mark-blessed-be-your-name-lyrics

Blessed be Your name when the sun's shining down on me
When the world's all as it should be
Blessed be Your name

And Blessed be Your name on the road marked with suffering
Though there's pain in the offering
Blessed be Your name

The Old Testament figure, Job, says it this way:

Naked I came from my mother's womb, and naked
shall I return there. The Lord gave and the Lord has
taken away. Blessed be the name of the Lord (Job 1:21).

Let us pray:

Dear Lord,

You never leave anyone alone to carry their troubles. I pray that You will give hope to those who are overwhelmed with trouble and who feel that they have no strength to go on.

I pray that You will heal the pain of those going through marriage problems and financial issues. For those who are suffering through illness and serious health problems, I pray for a complete healing, and may You give them peace as they wait on You.

I pray for Your strength to overcome for those who are dealing with addictions of every kind.

May You provide for those who need a job. I pray for favour and blessing on those who are struggling to keep their homes.

Bless and heal those who are suffering from mental problems and dementia.

I pray for the persecuted throughout the world. May You give them Your peace to endure.

Protect children everywhere who are hungry and sick.

I pray for all those who are imprisoned in other nations for their faith. May You, in Your own time, give them strength and bring them home.

I pray for the peace of Jerusalem and protection for Israel.

I pray for the welfare of Canada and affirmation of our Judeo-Christian roots while welcoming those of Islamic and other faith traditions.

Amen.

Chapter Four

Spiritual Needs of Older Adults

Literature provides numerous analogies in speaking of the human life cycle. Some writers have described life as a journey. Depending on the values of the particular society, life can be a journey to wealth and worldly success; a journey to noble, altruistic goals; or a journey to more spiritual and everlasting goals. All analogies based on the journey suggest that, like any journey, life will have its mountaintops and its low valleys, its deserts and its oases, its obstacles and its freeways.

Other writers have described life as a process—a process of birth, of growth, of renewal, of maturation, and of decline. Building on that analogy, I prefer to think of life as a growing season. With that end in view, there is a time and a purpose for every season in the life cycle. There is a time for planting—to prepare the soil and to plant the seed. There is a time for nurturing—to bask carefree in the sunshine and to soak up the cool spring rains. There is a time for renewal—to produce the seedlings for a new generation. There is a time for maturing—to grow straight and tall in the hot summer sunshine.

And, there is a time for harvesting—to reap the produce of our toil and to store it in the granaries in preparation for a long cold winter. We can approach the season of harvest with fear and trepidation, knowing not what the blizzards of winter will bring. Or, we can come to the harvest full of joy and thanksgiving—joy for a bountiful crop and thanksgiving for the blessings of the moments of sunshine and the time of rain.

I propose to you that life's season of harvest is a time to be celebrated, not feared. The harvest is to be enjoyed. It is a time during which we can share our good fortune. It is a time for sharing our wisdom and our experiences. It is a time for sharing the joy of a life well lived in spite of our weaknesses and in spite of our shortcomings. Robert Browning, in his poem titled "Rabbi Ben Ezra," rejoices in the celebration of life with his immortal words: *Grow old along with me! The best is yet to be, the last of life, for which the first was made.*

A wonderful gift that humans possess is the ability to recall and feast upon memories from the past. Precious moments from our past can be gathered up and stored as nourishment along the way in our later years. Like grain, those memories can be harvested and carried home into our barns. For, although our mortal body may age and grow frail, our spirit can stay young forever.

This apparent ambiguity is easier to state than it is to understand. One reason for that difficulty is that we have tended to view aging from an almost exclusively biological perspective. We have overlooked the fact that we are more than human beings having a spiritual experience. No. Far from it. We are spiritual beings having a human experience.

The following poem, *"You Tell Me I'm Getting Old"* by Dora Johnson[60], illustrates my point:

> You tell me I am getting old. I tell you that's not so!
> The house I live in is worn out, and that of course, I know.
> It's been in use a long, long while; it's weathered many a gale;
> I'm really not surprised you think it's getting somewhat frail.
> The color's changing on the roof, the window's getting dim.
> The walls are a bit transparent and looking rather thin.
> The foundation is not so steady as once it used to be.
> My house is getting shaky, but my house isn't me.
> My few short years can't make me old.
> I feel in my youth, eternity lies ahead, a life of joy and truth.
> I'm going to live forever there; life will go on, it's grand.
> You tell me I'm getting old, you just don't understand.
> The dweller in my little house is young and bright and gay;
> Just starting on a life to last throughout eternal day.
> You only see the outside, which is all that most folks see.
> You tell me I'm getting old, you've mixed my house with me.

Despite significant research in recent years, we often tend to fear aging, thinking of it as a downhill slide, a gradual decrease in vitality, and a not-so-gradual increase in vulnerability.

So, with that as a backdrop, let's turn now to what we mean when speaking of the spiritual. To some, the term "spiritual" refers to that which is without physical substance as compared to that which is bodily or material. With that view, if we, as human creatures, could

---

60 Davidson, Jim. (2019). *The best of Jim Davidson: Most requested selections from the author's nationally syndicated radio series.* Strategic Book Publishing and Rights Co. https://books.google.ca/books

be divided into compartments, then our physical needs, our mental needs, our emotional needs, and our social needs would be seen as co-existing alongside some other neat little compartment labelled "spiritual needs." Some might fill this "spiritual compartment" with religious devotions such as churchgoing, prayer, and religious devotions. In other words, that which is "spiritual" becomes a separate set of activities and a separate area of life as depicted in the following diagram.

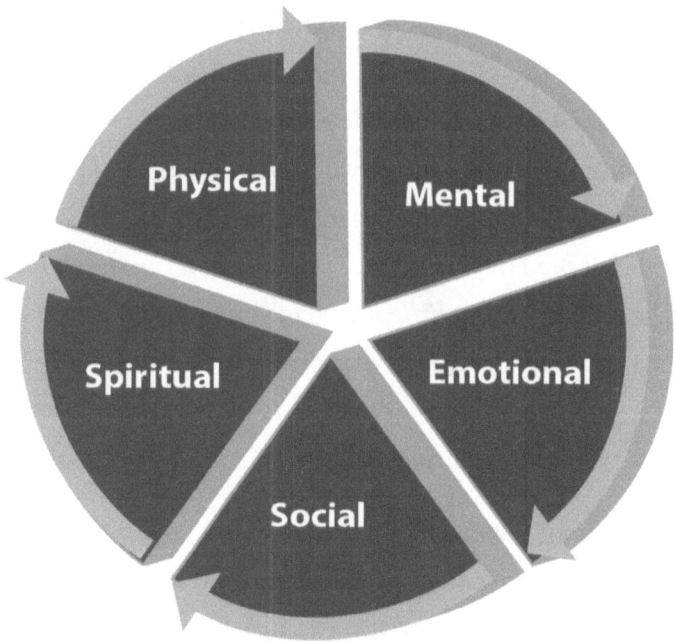

This is not this author's interpretation of the term "spiritual." Compartmentalizing will not be the focus of this text. Rather, by "spirituality," I am speaking of not one compartment of life, but the deepest dimension of all life, as depicted in the following illustration.

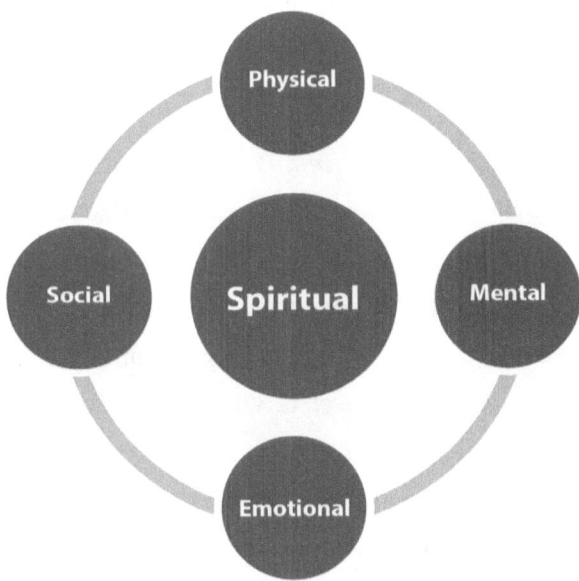

When I use the term "spiritual," it will be in reference to the ultimate ground of all our questions, all our hopes, all our dreams, and all our loves. For the older adult, it is the effort to deal creatively with retirement and to find a purpose—a goal—for one's life now that the family has been raised and the house has so much more space than is needed. It is the struggle with the loss of one's spouse, or the move from a home of many years and many memories. It is questions of self-worth and *raison d'être*. It is the apprehension of reaching out to initiate new friendships. It is the discovery of yet-to-be-revealed talents, deeper peace, and wider boundaries of love. All of these are spiritual concerns, for spirituality encompasses the entire human person in all of his or her needs, wishes, aspirations, and relationships.

This is consistent with the position advanced by the National Interfaith Coalition on Aging who, in defining spiritual well-being of older adults, concluded that:

> "At our core, we humans are spiritual beings. Spirituality can be viewed in a variety of ways from a traditional understanding of spirituality as an expression of religiosity, in search of the sacred, through to a humanistic view of spirituality devoid of religion. Health is also multi-faceted, with increasing evidence reporting the relationship of spirituality with physical, mental, emotional, social, and vocational well-being... Spiritual health is a dynamic state of being, reflected in the quality of relationships that people have in up to four domains of spiritual well-being: Personal domain where a person intra-relates with self; Communal domain, with in-depth inter-personal relationships; Environmental domain, connecting with nature; Transcendental domain, relating to something or someone beyond the human level. The Four Domains Model of Spiritual Health and Wellbeing embraces all extant worldviews from the ardently religious to the atheistic rationalist."[61]

Spirituality should be thought of as distinct from being associated with any organized religion. All the world's religions have a spirituality. It is also a common need among people who do not identify with any religion or defined religious practice(s).

---

61   National Interfaith Coalition on Aging. (1975). Spiritual well-being: A definition. *NICA.*

There is a multitude of definitions of spirituality. In addition to those identified above, a few explanations found in literature are:

1. Sister Joan Puls identifies that:

    Spirituality embraces all of life, breathes through its homely details and its noble intentions. It is at the heart of our efforts to be human. It is the seamless robe worn in all our roles. Spirituality arouses in us an awe for the mystery of every human life. It is the lived connection of body and spirit, work and play, life and death ... Perhaps most specifically, it is the degree of our harmony with all that is within us and without us. We become spiritual when we inhabit our bodies, know our own souls, and insert ourselves gracefully into all that surrounds us.[62]

    Puls goes on to identify that which is required if we are to achieve our spiritual goals. She says, "*Being spiritual demands the combined investment of our whole heart, our whole mind, our sexuality, our psyche, our sweat, and our very breath.*"[63] Now there is commitment.

2. Bede Griffiths, known by the end of his life as Swami Dayananda ("bliss of compassion"), offers a useful image of spirituality. Griffiths was a British-born Benedictine monk and priest who lived in ashrams in South India and became a noted Christian yogi.[64] He became a leading thinker in the development of the dialogue between Christianity and Hinduism. During an interview shortly before his death in 1993, when Griffiths was

---

62 Puls, Sr. Joan. (1985). Every bush is burning: a spirituality for our times. *World Council of Churches*.

63 Puls, Sr. Joan. (1985). Every bush is burning: a spirituality for our times. *World Council of Churches*.

64 Griffiths, B. (1984). *Christ in India: Essays towards a Hindu-Christian dialogue.* Templegate Publishers.

asked about the differences and similarities between various world religions, he spread out his hand. The religions are like the separate fingers, he said, and are quite distinct one from the other. For example, each has its own distinct revered teachers, sacred texts, dogmas, and rituals. But, Griffiths continued, if you trace each finger to its source, the palm of the hand, you see that the religions all come together in their depths.

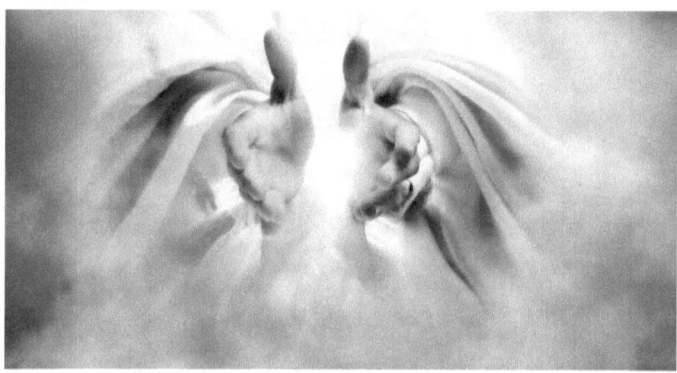

3. Thirteenth-century German mystic, Meister Eckhart, put it another way, calling God an underground river of wisdom with many wells tapping into it. That river is spirituality.

4. Jungian therapist Jeremiah Abrams defines spirituality as a holy longing, a yearning to know the meaning of our lives, to have a connection with the transpersonal.

5. Catholic educator Sr. Regina Coll suggests that spirituality is an *"awareness of the 'more than meets the eye' in our daily lives ... it refers to our hopes and dreams, our patterns of thought, our emotions, feelings, and behaviours."*[65]

---

65   Coll, Sr. Regina. (1993). *Christianity and feminism inc.* Twenty Third Publications.

6. Gerald May, a psychiatrist and director of spiritual guidance, seconds that view, linking the term to our deepest values and desires, the very core of our being.

7. Latin American liberation theologian Leonardo Boff calls spirituality *"that attitude which puts life at the center, and defends and promotes life against all the mechanisms of death, desiccation, or stagnation."*[66]

8. The journey toward wholeness is a common theme in some definitions of spirituality. For example, psychotherapist Molly Young Brown writes: *"When we expand our awareness, strengthen our center, clarify our purpose, transform our inner demons, develop our will, and make conscious choices, we are moving toward deeper connection with our spiritual self."*[67]

In summing up this discussion, I refer to Steindl-Rast and Lebell who provide one of the clearest explanations that I have encountered. They say:

> *Sometimes people get the mistaken notion that spirituality is a separate department of life, the penthouse of our existence. But rightly understood, it is a vital awareness that pervades all realms of our being. Someone will say, "I come alive when I listen to music," or "I come to life when I garden," or "I come alive when I play golf." Wherever we come alive, that is the area in which we are spiritual. And then we can say, 'I know at least how one is spiritual in that area.' To be vital,*

---

66 Boff, Leonardo. (2015). *Toward an eco-spirituality.* The Crossroad Publishing Company.
67 Brown, M. Y. (2009). *Growing whole: Self-realization for the great turning.* Psychosynthesis Press.

awake, aware, in all areas of our lives, is the task that
is never accomplished, but it remains the goal.[68]

Many definitions, subtle differences in emphasis. Each allows for spirituality to be an everyday adventure—a growing, coherent set of responses integrated into the complex patterns of human life.

Spiritual Needs

Based on more than 30 years of psychological counseling and pastoral care, Howard Clinebell[69] identified that humans share seven spiritual hungers.[70] They are:

- All people need to experience regularly the healing and empowerment of love from others, self, and an ultimate source/God.

- Everyone needs to experience renewing times of transcendence—moments that expand us beyond the immediate sensory spheres.

- Every person needs vital beliefs that give some sense of meaning and hope in the midst of losses, tragedies, and failures.

- Everyone needs to have values, priorities, and life commitments—usually centred in issues of justice, integrity, and love—that guide them in personally and socially responsible living.

---

68 Steindl-Rast, D., & Lebell, S. (2001). *Music of silence: A sacred journey through the hours of the day.* (2nd ed.). Ulysses Press.

69 Howard John Clinebell (1922–2005) was a minister in the United Methodist Church and a professor in pastoral counseling. Clinebell pioneered a counseling approach that combined psychotherapy and religion.

70 Clinebell, H. (1984). Basic Types of Pastoral Care and Counseling: resources for the ministry of healing and growth. Nashville: Abingdon Press.

- Each human being needs to discover and develop their inner wisdom, creativity, and love of their unique transpersonal/spiritual self.

- All people need a deepening awareness of oneness with other people and with the natural world, the wonderful web of all living things.

- Every human being needs spiritual resources to help heal the painful wounds of grief, guilt, resentment, unforgiveness, self-rejection, and shame. We also need spiritual resources to deepen our experiences of trust, self-esteem, hope, joy, and the love of life.

According to Clinebell, each of us, as human creatures, must pay attention to these needs if we are to feel whole and fulfilled, making spirituality central to human well-being.

Stallwood[71] defined a spiritual need as *"the lack of any factor or factors necessary to establish and/or maintain a dynamic, personal relationship with God."* Based on Stallwood's definition, Fish and Shelly[72] identified three basic spiritual needs—the need for meaning and purpose, the need for love and relatedness, and the need for forgiveness. To this, I would add a few more spiritual needs for the older adult. They include the need for hope, the need for life satisfaction, and the need to find closure for one's life. Let's look at each of these needs in greater detail.

---

71 Stallwood, J. (1975). In Beland and Passos (eds.) *Spiritual dimensions of clinical nursing.* (3rd ed.). McMillan.

72 Fish, S., & Shelly, J. A. (1983). *Spiritual Care: The Nurse's Role.* Intervarsity Press.

The Need for Meaning and Purpose

Regarding the need for meaning and purpose, Viktor Frankl[73] writes that our search for meaning is a primary force in life. Life is a task, writes Frankl, but the way in which people approach that task may differ. It is this difference in approach which will affect each individual's ability to cope with life's crises and to find meaning and purpose in those experiences.

According to Frankl, the difference between the religious and the apparently irreligious person is that the religious person experiences his or her existence not simply as a task, but as a mission. The religious person is aware of his or her taskmaster, the source of her or his mission. This can lead to a deeper relationship with God, to emotional and spiritual growth, and to the ability to reach out to help other people in their time of need.

Staying involved in the community is beneficial at any age. This is especially true for older adults. Many older adults crave meaningful involvement in their communities as a way to increase their social lives, bridge generation gaps, and feel that they are helping others. Volunteerism is one of the best ways to meet each of these goals while also keeping active. Volunteering also provides the added benefit of a flexible schedule, which allows time for oneself. Having an active role in the community can add purpose and meaning while building new and lasting friendships. Best of all, community involvement builds stronger and healthier communities in which we all thrive.

There is no doubt that, even after the end of their working lives, older adults continue to play an active and full role in society, contributing

---

73   Frankl, V. E. (1971). *Man's Search for Meaning*. Washington Square Press.

their knowledge and experience. Not only are they making a contribution to their community, but volunteering has significant benefits to one's physical, mental, and social health. To name a few, those personal and social benefits include an enhanced ability to keep fit; a healthy aging process; the contribution of their time, experience, and knowledge so they can feel useful; increased self-esteem; and the knowledge of contributing to helping others who are in need.

In short, all these factors converge on a single goal, which is to achieve active aging. Active aging is the most effective system for preventing premature dependence and extending optimal conditions for personal independence as long as possible, ensuring that older adults have a good quality of life, something which benefits society as a whole.

Like its potential benefits, the opportunities to be involved in our communities (however we define those to be) are limitless. A few examples of volunteerism for most any age or ability include:

- **Volunteer at a food bank**. Food banks collect and organize donated food before distributing it to those in need. Volunteers can help gather the food, organize and clean the stockroom, or work in the office.

- **Volunteer at a hospital or surgery centre**. These facilities often need volunteers to work at front desks or nurse's stations to provide information to visitors. Seniors often provide the cheery face and the empathy that is so dearly needed at local hospitals. Their compassion can be comforting to others in times of need.

- **Help at the local library or elementary school.** Typical duties include helping children find books to read, helping them with basic schoolwork, and being a friend. This type of volunteering goes a long way toward bridging a generation gap and can provide joy in the lives of both the children and the older adult.

- **Volunteer at a soup kitchen, homeless shelter, or animal shelter.** These organizations have ongoing needs that must be met for them to serve the community. Your helping hands will be much appreciated and will benefit others.

- **Handwrite thank-you notes for charities.** Reach out to any local charity and they will likely tell you that they need help keeping up with all their thank-you notes to donors! It's far more meaningful to get a handwritten note, but it also takes more time.

- **Read to children at the library.** Your local library's children's programs just might be in need of someone to lead one of these programs or volunteer every so often to read books and assist with crafts. It's a joy to be around children and watch them learn.

- **Volunteer at a church.** Volunteers are always needed to help with church outreach and other programs. Whatever your skill level or interest, the pastor and staff will be able to guide you to an activity that is enjoyable and fulfilling for you. Cleaning, decorating, data entry, leading a particular program, and more will greatly help the church serve more people in the community.

- **Make blankets or hats for newborn babies.** If you have a knack for knitting or crocheting, consider using these talents to make blankets or hats for newborn babies. Many hospitals have programs for underserved mothers and babies to help provide them with the essentials. Your hats and blankets will add the extra special touch of being homemade.

- **Contribute to a bake sale or soup sale.** Contribute to a bake sale or host your own! Choose a cause you care about and use the proceeds to benefit this cause. You will have fun baking and sampling your treats with friends and family. And best of all, you will be helping the community while you do it.

- **Plant flowers at a park.** Reach out to your local park and see if they have a volunteer program for maintaining its property. If not, start one! You and some friends can plant flowers, trim shrubs, and clean up the park. If you're not physically able to do lawn work, you can help by doing some crafts, such as painting pots for plants or rocks with colourful designs to decorate the park.

These, of course, are just a few examples of where you can make a difference in the lives of others while bringing meaning and purpose to your days. Volunteering should not feel like tedious work. If you're enjoying what you're doing, regardless of the task, then it shouldn't feel like work. Find the tasks you love doing and just have fun! The possibilities are endless.

Let us pray:

Father,

I know that You have a plan for each of our lives,
and that is for every one of Your children to know You
and to live our lives in a manner that is pleasing to You.

Help me to fulfill all that You would have me do in my life.
May I be obedient to Your voice as I seek to carry out Your
purpose for my life.
Help me to be filled with joy and to pray without ceasing.

Strengthen me to face the challenges of life.
Protect me from the urge to repay evil for evil
but rather love my enemy, and to do good to those who
would harm me.

Focus me so that I may more and more develop the Fruits
of the Holy Spirit
and may an abundance of love and joy,
peace and patience,
kindness and goodness,
faithfulness, gentleness, and self-control
overflow from my life into the lives of all whom I meet
until Christ is formed in me and I live my life as unto Him.

May I reflect Your purpose in my life
from this day forward to Your praise and glory.

This I ask in the name of Jesus my Saviour,

Amen.

The Need for Love and Relatedness

Fish and Shelly's second spiritual need, the need for love and related-ness, is fulfilled in the context of significant human relationships. Masumi Toyotome[74] writes that the security and satisfaction of being loved by someone is basic to a happy life. Toyotome identifies at least three kinds of love, which, he says, can determine a person's happiness in life. They are the "if" kind of love, the "because" kind of love, and the "in spite of" kind of love.

The "if" kind of love can be explained by the sentence: "If you satisfy my needs, then I will love you." It has strings attached—a conditional love motivated by self-interest. Love is not freely given. Rather, love has to be earned, and is given only after the person has "measured up" to the expectations of the other.

The "because" kind of love is reflected in statements such as: "I love you because of who you are." "I love you because of what you have." "I love you because of what you do." The burden of having to earn another's love is absent, but the fear of losing that love is ever-present, for what if I no longer have the very thing for which I am loved? For example, a man with paraplegia, a victim of a recent traffic accident, may feel the fear of no longer being able to measure up to his wife's expectations of the ideal husband—loved for what he has or does.

In contrast to the first two, the "in spite of" kind of love comes with no strings attached. It is a love that makes no demands other than that the other person be open to receive it. The spiritual and emotional growth which can result from an experience of this magnitude may not be immediately observable. And, it may not even be welcomed at the time.

---

74   Toyotome, M. (1961). *Three Kinds of Love*. Intervarsity Press.

But, it can be a powerful source of hope and courage for the future. For example, an older adult, faced with the decision to enter into a nursing home, could be in special need of the "in spite of" kind of love, and the relationships which reflect that love.

We find that same message, albeit in different phraseology, in St. Paul's First Letter to the Church at Corinth, when he says:

> *Love is patient; love is kind; love is not envious or boastful or arrogant or rude. It does not insist on its own way; it is not irritable or resentful; it does not rejoice in wrongdoing, but rejoices in the truth. It bears all things, believes all things, hopes all things, endures all things. Love never ends. But as for prophecies, they will come to an end; as for tongues, they will cease; as for knowledge, it will come to an end.*

> *For we know only in part, and we prophesy only in part; but when the complete comes, the partial will come to an end. When I was a child, I spoke like a child, I thought like a child, I reasoned like a child; when I became an adult, I put an end to childish ways. For now we see in a mirror, dimly, but then we will see face to face. Now I know only in part; then I will know fully, even as I have been fully known. And now faith, hope, and love abide, these three; and the greatest of these is love* (1 Corinthians 13:4–12).[75]

This reading, which has been translated into English from the original Greek, describes love as patient, kind, not envious or boastful or

---

75   Holy Bible: New Revised Standard Version. (1993). Catholic Bible Press.

arrogant or rude, not insisting on its own way, and not irritable or resentful. Love, St. Paul tells us, bears all things, believes all things, hopes all things, and endures all things. In the Greek language, love is spoken of as having different levels. Instead of one word, the Greek language breaks love down into four different—but related—words. Let's take a look at those four words.

The first is *eros*. This is the derivative of the English word *erotic*. *Eros* is focused on pleasure—one that is self-centred—focused on "what's in it for me." This is not the kind of love of which St. Paul is speaking.

The second word for love is *philia*, which refers to friendship—the love that binds two friends together. It describes a love that is based on mutual appreciation. It often says, "You scratch my back, and I'll scratch yours." *Philia* is not the love of which St. Paul is speaking.

The third word for love in the Greek language is *storge*. This is a word for affection. It is the love for family. *Storge* is the word used in referring to the love which parents have for their children. As tender as such love is, *storge* is not the love of which St. Paul is speaking.

The fourth kind of love—the kind of love of which St. Paul is speaking—is captured in the Greek word *agape*. *Agape* is the self-sacrificial love of Jesus, who loves us even when we are at our worst, even when we are most unlovable. *Agape* love is unconditional love. It knows no limits and sets no boundaries. *Agape* always gives, never expecting anything in return. When we love in the *agape* style, we always look for the well-being of those whom we love, placing their interests before our own.

Let us pray:

Father God,

I come into Your presence so aware of my human frailty and yet overwhelmed by Your love for me. You have created us to love and to be loved, with a deep and lasting love that is a mirror of the depth of love that Christ has for His Church.

Develop in me the depth of love that loves as Christ loved … a love that flows from You to us … a love that is to flow through us to others.

Father, I have fallen in and out of love. I pray that I may develop a new and extraordinary depth of love that comes only through You, so that at the right time You would bring into my life that kindred spirit and soul mate, whose love for me is only exceeded by their love of You.

I thank You that there is no human experience that I might walk through where Your love cannot reach me. If I climb the highest mountain, You are there, and yet, if I find myself in the darkest valley of my life, You are also there.

Teach me today to love You more. Help me to rest in that love that asks nothing more than the simple trusting heart of a child.

I ask this in the name of Jesus Christ, who loved me, and gave His life for me.
Amen.

The Need for Forgiveness

The third spiritual need, identified by Fish and Shelly, is the need for forgiveness. Guilt often develops from our failure to live up to either our own self-imposed expectations or the expectations of others. This perceived failure may not be due so much to our frailties and limitations as it is to unrealistic expectations (our own or others') imposed on us. Our perceived failures can create guilt.

It has been said that a guilty conscience is the seasoning of our daily lives, it is what keeps us honest. However, a guilty conscience can ultimately bring us to our knees. A person in need of forgiveness could be compared to a drowning man, flailing his arms around in a futile attempt to rescue himself, trying everything to keep his head above water. He is too dangerous for another swimmer to approach directly, for he will take the would-be-rescuer down with him. It is only when the drowning man stops trying to save himself, admits defeat in his own ability, and trusts enough to be still so that the friend who has jumped in to save him can come near. It is only then that he can be rescued. The drowning man must have faith in his rescuer. He must learn to trust that his rescuer is there for one purpose, and that is to bring him safely to shore.

Jesus says,

> Come to me, all you that are weary and are carry-ing heavy burdens, and I will give you rest. Take my yoke upon you, and learn from me; for I am gentle and humble in heart, and you will find rest for your souls. For my yoke is easy, and my burden is light (Matthew 11:28–29).

Who among us doesn't carry a burden? How many of us carry sorrow in our hearts for things we have done in the past? How many of us are angry about things that we cannot entirely let go? What about fear: fear of abandonment; fear of violence; fear of responsibility? Some of us are struggling with the death of a loved one, broken relationships, addictions, poor health, or problems at home or work. Each of us carry our own personal burdens.

What does Jesus say to us? *"Come to me … come to me … and I will give you rest."* Jesus has no intention of leaving us alone to carry our own burdens. *"Come to me,"* He says, and then He adds: *"Take my yoke upon you … and you will find rest … for my yoke is easy and my burden is light."*

We see that word "yoke" often in sacred Scripture. To help us understand why Jesus is using this symbol of a yoke, let's take a trip back into ancient Israel. Many of Jesus's listeners that day would have been devout Jews, and they were required to submit to the authority of Jewish law, the Torah. The Torah is the five books of Moses, the first five books of our sacred Scriptures: Genesis, Exodus, Leviticus, Numbers, and Deuteronomy. The Pharisees had identified 613 additional laws within the Torah. Laws about worship, cleanliness, marriage, nutrition, and most every other aspect of Jewish life.

In addition, every rabbi would have had his own expectations for his followers. His expectations were called "hedges," his suggested way of living, which he taught as his interpretation of the Torah. The rabbi's hedges, or expectations, were referred to as that particular rabbi's yoke, and every rabbi had his own distinctive yoke. Each rabbi's yoke was heavy with expected behaviours.

Jesus was also a rabbi, a Jewish teacher of the first century. He, too, had His own "rabbinic yoke." But Jesus's yoke is about our relationship with Him, as opposed to adherence to laws. Remember, Jesus says, "*my yoke is easy… my burden is light.*"

There is a second aspect to an ancient yoke which helps us to understand what Jesus is teaching us. A yoke was an important tool in an agrarian society. It was a harness, usually a wooden beam or frame that joined two oxen at the necks so they could work as a team pulling a load or a plough. Notice that it takes two animals to work a yoke. The farmer chose his oxen carefully. One of the animals was always more experienced than the other. The more experienced one was the leader, but both animals worked together to pull the load. It took both animals working together to accomplish the task.

Now, in sacred Scripture, the yoke is a symbol of being under the Lordship of Christ. Jesus says, "*Take my yoke upon you….*" The yoke belongs to Him and He invites each of us to be His yoke-mate. You see, the yoke of Christ is not just a yoke *from* Christ, but it is also a yoke *with* Christ. To take on Christ's yoke is to know that we are not bearing our burdens alone. We are bearing our burdens together with Christ and by the wisdom and the strength that comes from Him.

There is a poem, by an unknown poet, entitled "*Bike Ride with God*" which helps to illustrate this point. I've condensed it a bit and it goes like this:

> *For me, life with Christ was rather like a bike ride.*
> *But it was a tandem bike,*
> *And I noticed that Christ was always in the back helping me pedal*
> *when I needed an extra boost.*

I don't know just when it was ... that He suggested we change places.
But we did ... and life has not been the same since.
When I had control, I thought I knew where I was headed.
My life, for the most part, was predictable.

But when Jesus took the lead ... and I was anxious about things
He would lean back and touch my hand ... and say ...
"Just pedal."

I did not trust Him, at first, being in control of my life.
I thought He'd wreck it.
But Jesus knows bike secrets.
Knows how to make it bend to take sharp corners,
Knows how to jump to clear high rocks.

I am learning to be content ... pedaling in the strangest places.
And I'm beginning to enjoy the view,
with my constant companion, Jesus Christ.

And when I'm feeling overwhelmed ... and I'm sure I just can't do
it anymore,
He smiles and says ...
"Just pedal."

My brothers and sisters in Christ, this reading gives us the imagery of Jesus and you and Jesus and me yoked together, pulling the load together, bearing our burden together. Whatever trials or burdens come your way, Jesus is there right beside you guiding you and helping to shoulder your burdens. So, when you are feeling overwhelmed and heavily burdened, remember those two small words: *just pedal*, and let Jesus be your guide. This is how the yoke becomes easy and the burden light.

Let us pray:

> Lord Jesus, through the power of the Holy Spirit,
> Go back into my memory.
> Every hurt that has ever been done to me, please heal
> that injury.
> Every hurt that I have ever caused another person, please
> heal that person's injury.
>
> All the relationships that have been damaged in my life,
> whatever the cause, please heal those relationships.
>
> But, Lord, if there is something which I need to do, if I need
> to go to a person who is still suffering from my hand or my
> careless words, bring to my awareness that person.
>
> I choose to forgive.
> And, I ask to be forgiven.
>
> Remove whatever bitterness may be in my heart, Lord, and
> fill the empty spaces with Your love.
>
> Amen.

The Need for Hope

In times of doubt, in times of trials, in times of difficulty and despair, our fundamental beliefs about God and our faith are challenged. How can we find faith in the midst of our doubts? How can we trust

God's plan when our lives seem out of His control, and prayers seem to go unanswered, or, as it feels sometimes, even unheard?

How? With trust in the omnipotent power of our Lord and King; with hearts full of hope.

Hope, in its widest definition, is described as *"the desire of something together with the expectation of obtaining it."*[76] It is a movement of the appetite toward a future good, which, though hard to attain, is actually attainable.

The Catechism of the Catholic Church defines a virtue as *"a habitual and firm disposition to do the good."*[77] In Holy Mother Church's Catechism, hope is one of three theological virtues that have been infused in us (or given as gifts to us) by God, as is true of the other two essentially infused virtues, faith and charity (or love).

The theological virtues relate directly to our relationship with Father God. The theological virtues adapt our faculties for participation in the divine nature by disposing Christians to live in a relationship with the Trinity. These virtues are *"infused by God into the souls of the faithful to make them capable of acting as his children and of meriting eternal life."*[78]

Hope, specifically, is defined as *"the theological virtue by which we desire the kingdom of heaven and eternal life as our happiness, placing our trust in Christ's promises and relying not on our own strength,*

---

76   https://www.catholic.com/encyclopedia/hope

77   Canadian Conference of Catholic Bishops. (2000). *Catechism of the Catholic Church.* CCC #1803.

78   Canadian Conference of Catholic Bishops. (2000). *Catechism of the Catholic Church.* CCC #1812.

but on the help of the grace of the Holy Spirit."[79] *"The virtue of hope responds to the aspiration to happiness which God has placed in the heart of every man; it takes up the hopes that inspire men's activities and purifies them so as to order them to the Kingdom of heaven; it keeps man from discouragement; it sustains him during times of abandonment; it opens up his heart in expectation of eternal beatitude. Buoyed up by hope, he is preserved from selfishness and led to the happiness that flows from charity."*[80]

In his letter to the Hebrews, St. Paul tells us, *"We have this hope, a sure and steadfast anchor of the soul, a hope that enters the inner shrine behind the curtain, where Jesus, a forerunner on our behalf, has entered, having become a high priest forever according to the order of Melchizedek"* (Hebrews 6:19–20). My friends, it is hope which affords joy even when (or especially when) we are under trial. Hope has, as its main objective, our union with God in heaven.

If spirituality is a journey toward some goal, then the essence of spirituality must be hope. Marcel[81] identified that *"Hope means first accepting the trial as an integral part of the self..."* Marcel discussed two characteristics of the phenomenon of hope that may be of particular importance to understanding the spiritual needs of older adults. The first is that, *"there can strictly speaking be no hope except when the temptation to despair exists"* and, secondly, that *"hope... involves a fundamental relationship of consciousness to time."*

---

79   Canadian Conference of Catholic Bishops. (2000). *Catechism of the Catholic Church.* CCC #1817.

80   Canadian Conference of Catholic Bishops. (2000). *Catechism of the Catholic Church.* CCC #1818.

81   Marcel, G. (1962). *Homo viator: Introduction to a metaphysic of hope.* (E. Craufurd, Trans.). Harper.

Spirituality, as a process, aims at the clarification of life. Its meaning may be much the same for both young and old alike. What does differ significantly is the *relationship of consciousness to time*, that is, the location in the life continuum in which the older adult finds herself or himself. The young person stands at the beginning of the life continuum with much of their journey yet to be experienced. The older adult, on the other hand, stands closer to the end of the continuum, with much of their journey behind them, and a heightened sensitivity to his or her own mortality. For the young, time provides the opportunity for increased engagement in life. For the aging person, time may be perceived as the impending separation from life.

If this is the case for the older adult, then despair could best be understood as the consciousness of time closing. Hope, on the other hand, aims to reunite, to recollect, to reconcile. With hope, time, however short it may be, is seen as full of opportunity and possibility.

When I think of hope-filled doubt in sacred Scripture, my thoughts turn to the first time Jesus appeared to His disciples after His resurrection. They were gathered in the Upper Room, with windows shuttered and doors locked, "for fear of the Jews" (John 20:19). One disciple, Thomas, was not there. Later, the disciples told Thomas they had seen the risen Lord. Thomas questioned Jesus's appearance, saying, "*Unless I see the mark of the nails … and put my hand into his side, I will not believe*" (John 20:25).

A week later, Jesus appeared to the disciples once again. This time, Thomas was present. And, we hear that Jesus showered His divine mercy on Thomas.

It's noteworthy that when we hear about Jesus's disciples, certain adjectives or descriptors come to mind. When we think of Judas, we think about betrayal. When we think of Peter, we might think of the Rock upon which Christ built His Church. When we think of John, we think of the disciple whom Jesus loved. And when we think of Thomas, we think about doubt or skepticism.

Personally, I think that Thomas gets a bum rap. Whenever we hear about Thomas, we don't just hear "Thomas," we always hear "*doubting Thomas*," as if there were several Thomases in the Bible and we somehow have to attach the adjective—doubting—to ensure that we have the right Thomas. Trust me here! Thomas, the Twin, is the only Thomas in the Bible.

I want us to take a moment to look at the man whom all too often we think of as "*doubting Thomas*." Was that his only characteristic? A man filled with doubt? Or did his inquiring mind have a purpose? Was Thomas's doubt really nothing less than his desire for hope?

In his Gospel, St. John mentions the disciple Thomas several times. Outside of the listing of the disciples' names, the first we hear about Thomas is in John's account of the raising of Lazarus (John 11:1–45). You know the story. Jesus is headed to Bethany because His good friend Lazarus is close to death. Bethany is a sleepy little village in the hill country of Judea. The last time that Jesus was in the hill country, the Jewish authorities had tried to seize Him and have Him killed. So, the disciples are not eager to go to Bethany, because there is a very real possibility that Jesus, and even the disciples themselves, could be arrested and put to death.

However, Thomas speaks up and says that he is willing to go to Bethany, even if it means dying with Jesus (John 11:16). You see, Thomas was putting into action what Christ had been teaching. Thomas was willing to follow the Master, even unto death. Thomas was determined to be faithful. So, I wonder, instead of calling him "*doubting Thomas*," why don't we call him "*ready-to-die-with-the-Lord Thomas?*"

The next mention that we find of Thomas is in Chapter 14 of John's Gospel. It goes like this:

> *In my Father's house there are many dwelling-places. If it were not so, would I have told you that I go to prepare a place for you?... And you know the way to the place where I am going." Thomas said to him, 'Lord, we do not know where you are going. How can we know the way?'* (John 14:2–5).

Thomas's question gives rise to one of Jesus's great *I AM* statements. Jesus replies to Thomas saying, "*I AM the way and the truth and the life.*" One of the best-known statements in Christianity stems from a question asked by Thomas. "*Lord, we do not know where you are going. How can we know the way?*" If Jesus is going someplace, Thomas wants to go with Him. So, instead of calling him "*doubting Thomas*," why don't we call him "*loyal Thomas?*"

We find the next passage about Thomas in the Gospel according to St. John, Chapter 21. The disciples are in a boat, fishing on the Sea of Galilee. The resurrected Christ appears on the shore. Despite the distance between them, Thomas is the first to recognize the Lord and he points Jesus out to the others. So, instead of calling him *"doubting Thomas,"* why don't we call him *"eagle eye Thomas?"*

In our world today, to call someone a *"doubting Thomas"* is a way of belittling him or her. If you're a *"doubting Thomas,"* people think you're someone who won't believe things, even when everyone else around you believes. If you're a *"doubting Thomas,"* people think you need to be persuaded because you don't have faith.

Is there anything in St. John's Gospel readings that suggest that Thomas did not have a strong faith? No, I don't believe so. After all, whose faith is greater: the one who never doubts? Or the faith that doubts and investigates, and then believes?

Thomas is not about doubt—far from it, he is filled with hope. Thomas needed to find out for himself. Thomas needed to believe, not because other people told him to believe, but because he needed the truth which only God Himself could reveal. Thomas needed hope, the kind of hope that could only be found by placing his trust in Christ's promises and relying not on his own strength, but on the grace of the Holy Spirit.

John's Gospel tells us that when Thomas touches the wounds of Jesus's crucifixion—Jesus' hands, His feet, and His side—Thomas responds with a firm and powerful statement of faith: *"My Lord and my God"* (John 20:28). Thomas's response is known as one of the clearest statements of faith that we find anywhere in sacred Scripture.

Thomas is a source of encouragement for all of us who struggle sometimes with church teachings and matters of faith. If we emphasize Thomas's doubt, then we miss the point. Because the punch line of the story—the real message it contains—is a message about Thomas's faith in Jesus as the One in whom we see the face of God.

I believe that, like Thomas, each one of us has our moments of doubt and moments of disbelief. Conscious of those moments of doubt, and conscious of our incredible need for hope, we are invited to place our hands into the wounds of Christ so that our faith, too, might be strengthened.

The Liturgy of the Most Holy Eucharist provides a fitting opportunity for Christ to touch our hearts. The next time you come forward to receive at the Table of the Lord, may you, like Thomas, be strengthened to proclaim: "My Lord and My God."

In the meantime, be encouraged by the words of Rufus Jones, a pastor of a century past, who put it this way:

> "A rebuilt faith is superior to an inherited faith that has never stood the strain of a great testing storm. If you have not clung to a broken piece of your old ship in the dark night of the soul, your faith may not have the sustaining power to carry you through to the end of the journey."[82]

My friends, when you're feeling dizzy and disoriented because of doubt, remember Pastor Jones's observation. As you emerge from your uncertainties, I believe that you will possess a hardier faith, a deeper faith, and a more resilient, enduring, and hope-filled faith than you did before it was put to the test.

---

82   Strobel, Lee (2009). *God's Outrageous Claims: Thirteen Discoveries That Can Transform Your Life*. Zondervan.

Let's close with that famous traditional Celtic hymn, the lyrics of which were written by Jan Struther some 90 years ago. *"Lord of All Hopefulness,"*[83] it goes like this:

> *Lord of all hopefulness, Lord of all joy,*
> *Whose trust, ever child-like, no cares can destroy,*
> *Be there at our waking, and give us, we pray,*
> *Your bliss in our hearts, Lord, at the break of the day.*

> *Lord of all eagerness, Lord of all faith,*
> *Whose strong hands were skilled at the plane and the lathe,*
> *Be there at our labors, and give us, we pray,*
> *Your strength in our hearts, Lord, at the noon of the day.*

> *Lord of all kindliness, Lord of all grace,*
> *Your hands swift to welcome, your arms to embrace,*
> *Be there at our homing, and give us, we pray,*
> *Your love in our hearts, Lord, at the eve of the day.*

> *Lord of all gentleness, Lord of all calm,*
> *Whose voice is contentment, whose presence is balm,*
> *Be there at our sleeping, and give us, we pray,*
> *Your peace in our hearts, Lord, at the end of the day.*

Let us pray:

> Heavenly Father,
> I come before You today in need of hope.

---

83   https://hymnary.org/text/lord_of_all_hopefulness_lord_of_all_joy

At times, I feel helpless.
At times, I feel weak.

I pray for hope...
Hope for a brighter future.
Hope for a better life.
Hope for love and kindness.

It has been said that it is always darkest before the dawn.
I pray that is true, for all seems dark right now.
I pray to be filled with Your light.
To bask in Your glory.

When I lose hope because my plans have come to nothing,
remind me that Your love is always greater than
my disappointment.
Remind me that Your plans for my life are always better
than my dreams.

In Your name, I pray.
Amen.

The Need for Life Satisfaction

Aging is an interpersonal process, a fact that is often overlooked. People age in a social context as well as a physical one. Older adults are confronted with the beliefs, attitudes, and values about aging that exist throughout society. Older adults encounter expectations about what they are expected to feel and how they should conduct themselves. We have spoken of this in previous chapters.

Within this greater social context, a few life satisfaction scales for aging populations have been developed over the years. From those scales, several life satisfaction measures have been developed, and they include:

- taking pleasure in daily activities,

- regarding life as meaningful,

- goodness-of-fit between desired and achieved goals,

- positive mood,

- positive self-concept,

- satisfaction with perceived health status,

- satisfaction with one's financial security, and

- satisfaction with the number and quality of one's social contacts.

It is my opinion that many of these factors are also spiritual needs in and of themselves.

Let us pray:

> Oh Lord,
> You are my shepherd and I should not be in want,
> but so often I struggle to be content and I do want,
> forgetting that you have graciously provided me with every
> spiritual blessing and everything I need for life.

Thank you for often not giving me what I want,
because my desires would draw my heart from being satisfied in You.
Help me to be content with what You have given me
and to not be focused on what my flesh wants
or the world tells me I should have.

Protect me from coveting possessions or people,
talent or influence, relationships or prestige.
Keep my heart from being anxious for what I don't have,
and make me thankful for the numerous gifts that You have
already given.

Fill me with the joy and satisfaction of contentment
in Christ.
Help me learn to be content in any situation
and to quickly reject the idolatry
that dwells beneath the surface of my coveting.

I ask you to continually bring to mind Your faithful
provision for all of my needs,
that Christ died for my salvation,
that in Christ I am free to be satisfied.

In the name of Your son, Jesus, I pray.
Amen.

The Need to Find Closure to One's Life

If we are to understand life closure, we need to remember that death is a feature of all life forms on this planet. Human beings are no exception. Ultimately, each one of us must confront our own death. As misunderstood as death may be, it does somehow reaffirm the meaning of life.

There is a scene in the motion picture *The Man from Snowy River* in which a young man, Jim Craig, laments the accidental death of his father. The rough-hewn philosopher, Spooner, brings the young man sharply back to reality with the terse comment, "*There's more to life than death, Jim.*" That is certainly true. For most of us, concern for the quality of our life is of a more pressing nature than is our concern for things that have to do with our death. But, eventually, the quality of our death becomes top priority for each one of us.

Fear, or death anxiety, is the psychological state most often mentioned by researchers when discussing respondents' attitudes toward death. Death anxiety is a feeling of dread, apprehension, or anxiety which arises when one thinks of the process of one's death or dying. Some admit to this fear, some claim to be indifferent, and a few people actually welcome death.

Research abounds on the association between religion and death anxiety, but the findings are inconclusive, to say the least. Every possible relationship between the variables of religiosity and the fear of death has been reported in the literature, ranging from strongly positive to strongly negative to no correlation whatsoever. This is understandable. For any answer to death that an individual finds satisfactory will depend, in short, on the individual's attitude toward life, as well as the intensity of his or her fear of death and the kind of death being anticipated.

For some people, a genuine reconciliation with death may not be possible. Yet, for others, almost any argument may modify their apprehension toward death and lessen their despair. Further, an answer to death found to be consoling at one moment in time may be totally rejected at another point in time. Thus, there can be no universal answer to death, least of all a universally acceptable one.

Pherigo[84] identifies three of the more well-known explanations for reconciling a person's death. Each has arisen from its own unique background: one from a belief in Fatalism, one from a *"will-of-God"* theology, and one from the *"wearing-out"* syndrome. The history of Fatalism is derived from popular theology in ancient Greece. In post-Homer days, three old women, "the Fates," were believed to determine each person's life span. Human lives were imagined to be spun out, as if on spinning wheels. Even the gods were powerless to change the fatal decree. This belief, although no longer associated with Greek mythology, remains popular to this day. It surfaces in clichés such as *"what will be, will be"* and in ideas such as *"it must have been his time to go"* or *"if it isn't my time to die, nothing can kill me; if it is, nothing can save me."*

In the will-of-God explanation, it is believed that it is our Creator who determines our moment of death. The will-of-God approach ascribes the course of one's personal history to a controlling God. How we live our lives, health conscious or otherwise, will not lengthen

---

84   Pherigo, L. P. (1987). Death: The inevitable issue. In D. B. Oliver (ed.). *New directions in religion and aging.* Haworth Press.

our time in this world or our departure from it. In this explanation, God determines the moment when He will call us home.

The wearing-out theme is the third explanation. In our time, it appears to be the more popular one. We know that manufactured things have planned obsolescence. They wear out. It is not a quantum leap, then, to transfer a familiar known, such as an appliance's planned obsolescence, to an unknown that seems to have some parallels. Thus, it is thought that, over time, our vital organs simply wear out. Hence, we hear the explanation for an older adult having difficulty standing from a kneeling position, *"I am just getting old. My knees are wearing out."*

If this is the case, however, we are now living in a time when our medical profession should be able to replace our vital organs as they wear out. Successful organ transplants have become commonplace. Are we far away from a time when we will be able to create the parts which we need and, thereby, create the illusion that we can outwit death altogether?

It is my belief that life as we know it hardly deserves an eternal status. Death has its proper place not as the enemy, but as the final friend. As Christians, we believe in life after death. So, I want to share with you a story adapted from the third edition of Chicken Soup for the Soul. It goes like this:

> *The sound of Anna's voice on the other end of the tele-*
> *phone always brought a smile to Father Jim's face. Aunt*
> *Annie, as all the children called her, just seemed to be*
> *filled with joy wherever she went. This time, however,*
> *Fr. Jim sensed a certain anxiety in her words. "Father*

Jim, could you stop by this afternoon? I need to talk with you." His response: "Of course. I'll be there around three. Is that okay?"

As they sat in the quiet of Anna's living room, Fr. Jim learned the reason for the seriousness which he had sensed in her voice. Anna told him about her visit to the doctor. The tests had revealed a fast-growing tumour. "He says I probably have six months to live," she said.

Despite the seriousness of Anna's words, there was a definite calm about her. Fr. Jim started, "I'm so sorry to..." but before he could finish, Anna interjected. "Don't be. I have lived a good life. I'm ready to go. You know that.

"But I do want to talk with you about my funeral. I have been thinking about it, and there are some things that I know I want." They sat there for most of the afternoon, talking about Anna's favourite hymns, the scripture passages that had meant so much to her through the years, and the memories the two of them had shared.

When it seemed that they had covered just about everything, Anna paused, looking up at Fr. Jim with a twinkle in her eye, "One more thing, preacher," she said. "When they bury me, I want my old Bible in one hand and a fork in the other."

When asked why she wanted to be buried with a fork, Anna explained: "I've been thinking about all of the church dinners and banquets that I attended through the years. I couldn't begin to count them all. But one thing sticks in my mind.

"At those really nice get-togethers, when the main course was finished, a server would come by to collect the dirty dishes. Sometimes, he or she would lean over my shoulder and whisper, 'You can keep your fork.' And do you know what that meant? Dessert was coming! It didn't mean a cup of Jell-O or pudding or even a dish of ice cream. You don't need a fork for that. No! It meant the good stuff, something substantial, like chocolate cake or pumpkin pie! When they told me I could keep my fork, I knew the best was yet to come!

"That's exactly what I want people to talk about at my funeral. Oh, they can talk about all the good times we had together. That would be nice. But when they walk by my casket and see me there with a fork in my hand, I want them to wonder: What's with the fork?

"And I want you to tell them that I kept my fork because the best is yet to come. I want you to tell them, 'Something better is coming for you, so keep your fork too.'"

My brothers and sisters in Christ, the next time you are sitting at your dinner table and you reach down for your fork, let it remind you ever so gently that there is something better coming. Today, let this story remind you that when life in this world ends something better is coming. Jesus says, "*I go to prepare a place for you. And, I will come again and will take you to myself… so that where I am, there you may be also*" (John 14:3).

Let us pray:

> Father God,
> We thank You for the blessings of the seasons, for the beauty of this world, and for the gift of one another.
>
> Open our eyes, that we might see what You want us to see.
> Open our ears, that in our conversations, we might hear what You want us to hear.
> Open our hearts, that we might feel as You feel toward each one of our brothers and sisters.
>
> Heavenly Father, help us remember that the jerk who cut us off in traffic last week is a single mother who worked nine hours that day and is rushing home to cook dinner, help with homework, do the laundry, and spend a few precious moments with her children.
>
> Help us to remember that the pierced, tattooed, disinterested young man at the corner store who can't make change correctly is a worried 19-year-old university student, balancing his apprehension over a new school with his fear of not getting his student loans approved.

Remind us, Lord, that the scary looking derelict, begging for money in the same spot every day, is a slave to addictions that we can only imagine in our worst nightmares.

Help us to remember that the older couple walking annoyingly slow through the store aisles and blocking our shopping progress are savouring this moment, knowing that, based on the biopsy report he got back last week, this may be the last time that they go shopping together.

Heavenly Father, remind us each day that, of all the gifts you give us, the greatest gift is love. Open our hearts not just to those who are close to us, but to all of humanity. Let us be slow to judge and quick to forgive.

Lord, make my life a window for Your light to shine through and a mirror to reflect Your love to each person I meet.

I ask this in the name of the Lord Jesus Christ.
Amen.[85]

---

85 Adapted from https://www.beliefnet.com/prayers/protestant/compassion/help-us-remember.aspx

Chapter Five

Factors affecting the Religious
Practices of Older Adults

Organized religion and spiritual practices play a vital role in many people's lives, and this may be especially true for older adults. More than 90% of older adults identify themselves as being religious and/or spiritual. In fact, older adults have higher levels of religious commitment and participation than any other age group.[86]

For older adults in particular, there is a growing body of research that religious and spiritual practices may be positively associated with improved physical and mental health, increased longevity, and stronger social support systems. Older adults who identified themselves as religious and/or spiritual literally live longer. This may be due, in part, to the fact that religious and/or spiritual people tend

---

86   McFadden, S. H. (1996). Religion, spirituality, and aging. In J. E. Birren & K. Warner Schaie (eds.). *Handbook of the psychology of aging* (4th ed.), p. 162–177. Academic Press.

to exercise more, eat healthier, smoke less, use their seat belts, and attend preventive screenings.[87]

Researchers caution that there are limitations to the conclusions anyone should draw from these studies. It could be that people who attend religious services benefit from the social network they form. It might be that people in churches, synagogues, and mosques watch out for others, especially older adults, encouraging them, for example, to get help if they look sick. As well, religious beliefs or a strong feeling of spirituality outside of traditional religion may improve an individual's ability to cope with the stresses of everyday life and the challenges of aging. Or, it could be that certain personality types cope better with life and those are the types of people who also attend religious services more regularly.

The message here is not *"Go back to church and you'll live a long time,"* but rather, *"stay connected with people who are on your wavelength."* This could mean, for example, joining small prayer groups not associated with any particular religious institution, taking time for personal meditation, writing your life story, remaining optimistic about life even if age and illness take their toll, or forging social connections with family, friends, and others.

Religion and spirituality are not the same thing, although they do have similarities. Religion is based on a set of standards of beliefs and practices. For example, those who practice a specific religion may be expected to attend church, synagogue, or mosque on certain days; refrain from eating certain foods at certain times; or prepare

---

87   Merck and Company. (2016). *Merck manual: Religion and spirituality in older people.* Retrieved from http://www.merckmanuals.com/home/older-people%E2%80%99s-health-issues/social-issues-affecting-older-people/religion-and-spirituality-in-older-people

foods only in religiously acceptable ways. Religion involves rituals as well as teachings.

There are several factors which affect the manner in which older adults practice their faith in a Supreme Being. Determinants include such factors as age, gender, marital status, personal health status and functional independence, the health status and functional independence of one's spouse, and the significance of religion in one's younger life. Let's look at some of those factors in greater detail.

Age

In their review of studies concerned with age and religion, Argyle and Beit-Hallahmi[88] suggested that while frequency of church attendance tends to decrease after age 60, religious beliefs tend to increase. Blazer and Palmore[89] found evidence in a longitudinal study to support the suggestion of decreasing religious activity in later life (after age 70, on average), but concluded that religious attitudes were relatively stable during the same period.

Along the same vein, Gray and Moberg[90] suggested that a decrease in community-based religious practices, such as church attendance, may be counterbalanced by an increase in home-based religious practices, such as Bible reading or private prayer. Apparent declines in religious activity in the later years do not necessarily mean that religiosity is decreasing. Far from it; there is ample research that

---

88 Argyle, M., & Beit-Hallahmi, B. (1975). *The social psychology of religion*. Routledge & Kegan Paul.
89 Blazer, D., & Palmore, E. (1976). Religion and aging in a longitudinal panel. *The gerontologist*, 16, 82–84.
90 Gray, R. M., & Moberg, D. O. (1977). *The church and the older person*. Eerdmans, 91.

religious belief and activity remain relatively stable over time and, further, that both orthodoxy of beliefs and frequency of religious activity increase in the later years.

When I think of advancing age as an indicator of religious practice, I am reminded of a passage from Psalm 92, which says:

> *The righteous flourish like the palm tree, and grow like a cedar in Lebanon.*
> *They are planted in the house of the Lord; they flourish in the courts of our God.*
> *In old age they still produce fruit; they are always green and full of sap, showing that the Lord is upright; he is my rock, and there is no unrighteousness in him.*[91]

These verses offer the rich image of the righteous person as a tree, but not just any tree. No, a tree transplanted in the temple courts, protected from exposure to violent winds. God's eye is always upon you. His love surrounds you. And you are safe from those who would harm you.

On one level, the symbolism is fairly straightforward. Trees are symbolic of enduring life and fertility. Trees are long lived, in contrast to the grasses and plants of the field, which grow for a season only to wither and fade. Fittingly then, this text declares that those who are right with God will enjoy a similar long and fruitful life.

The interpreter should not fail, however, to notice that the trees described by the psalmist do not spring up just anywhere: "*They are planted in the house of the Lord; they flourish in the courts of our God.*" These long-lived, fruitful trees are planted and cultivated. They are

---

91   Holy Bible: New Revised Standard Version. (1993). Catholic Bible Press.

deliberately placed and nourished. Because of this care, they are able to flourish.

The symbolism is that God, in His grace, has drawn you close to Himself. You are in a place of honour. You are in a place of protection. God's promise relates to all of life and especially to old age. You are meant to flourish and grow. Your faith and your spiritual insight should increase. Your love and compassion for other people should grow richer and deeper. Your hope in God's plan for your future should become more intense.

And then, of course, one of the things a healthy, green tree does is bear fruit, even in old age. Date palms that are a hundred years old can still produce dates. Olive trees can grow to be much older and still produce fruit. Did you know that, on average, an olive tree will live 300 to 600 years? So, the psalmist is saying that, if you are righteous, in your old age you will be like a tree that stays fresh and green. You will be spiritually healthy. And you will bear much fruit.

What kind of fruit? In St. Paul's Letter to the Colossians, he speaks of "*bearing fruit in every good work as you grow in the knowledge of God*" (Colossians 1:10). And in his letter to the Galatians, St. Paul lists the qualities that are "*the fruit of the Spirit*": "*love, joy, peace, patience, kindness, goodness, faithfulness, gentleness, and self-control*" (Galatians 5:22–23).

So, the message is if you are a righteous person, God promises that in old age you will be spiritually alive and spiritually healthy, and you will produce spiritual fruit. You will stay fresh and green, proclaiming, "*The LORD is upright; he is my Rock, and there is no unrighteousness in him.*"

Let us pray:

> Jesus, my Friend,
> As my time in this world draws to a close
> and my energies decrease,
> more than ever, help me to be comforted in Your
> warm embrace.
>
> Give me strength to work in Your Service,
> to labour in Your vineyard until I draw my final breath.
> Help me to inspire others ... to encourage others
> as I walk into the dawn of eternity.
>
> Remind me that old age is not the twilight of a life
> well lived.
> Rather, it is the doorway to a brand-new day about to begin.
> It is the awakening, not the sleeping.
> It is the entrance to eternity, not death at work.
>
> It is that precious moment before the lifting of the Final Veil
> that shades me from Your Face, O God.
> May I go rejoicing in that vision,
> never to be separated from You.
>
> Amen.

Gender: Female

The literature suggests that gender is a factor in the personal expression of religiosity. Blazer and Palmar[92] concluded that women generally are significantly more religious than men in both their activities and their attitudes. These authors support the view that religiosity among older adults has a direct and positive relationship with one's sense of well-being, happiness, life satisfaction, and successful adjustment in aging.

Such findings are consistent with the conventional roles played earlier in life by men and women in this particular cohort. The man, as the "breadwinner," was responsible for ensuring the financial security of the family—bringing home the bacon, if you will. He had a great deal of emotional investment tied up in his job. Adequate financial status, for the older man, may generally reflect his sense of success in both his family and his employment roles.

For the woman in this age cohort, the home, family life, and social activities have traditionally been of primary concern. It is not unreasonable, then, to conclude that social support (and that includes the communal aspect of organized religious activities) would continue to provide a greater sense of well-being for the older woman.

When I think about the devoutness of women, my thoughts move to the resurrection of our Lord. In the Holy Gospel according to St. Luke (24: 1–9), we read:

> But on the first day of the week, at early dawn, they
> came to the tomb, taking the spices that they had

---

92 Blazer, D., & Palmore, E. (1976). Religion and aging in a longitudinal panel. *The Gerontologist*, 16, 82–84.

prepared. They found the stone rolled away from the tomb, but when they went in, they did not find the body. While they were perplexed about this, suddenly two men in dazzling clothes stood beside them. The women were terrified and bowed their faces to the ground, but the men said to them, "Why do you look for the living among the dead? He is not here, but has risen. Remember how he told you, while he was still in Galilee, that the Son of Man must be handed over to sinners, and be crucified, and on the third day rise again." Then they remembered his words, and returning from the tomb, they told all this to the eleven and to all the rest.

The women who went to the tomb on that very first Easter morning had been accompanying Jesus and His disciples for some time. They would have witnessed His teachings and the events of the previous weeks.

Imagine the scene: a small group of grieving women had gathered together to prepare Jesus's body for burial. It was a job that had been delayed so that they were able to faithfully celebrate the Passover, a significant Jewish festival.

The women probably gathered early in the morning in the village, bringing all the necessary spices and materials required for the task at hand. They would have been familiar with what was needed and what was to be done for the task of preparing bodies for burial because it was, after all, women's work. Once all the women had assembled, they would have set off from the village to the tomb of

Joseph of Arimathea, where Jesus's body had been laid. On the road, they would have been reminiscing and comforting each other.

As the women were familiar with the task at hand, they would have known what to expect. However, what they found was nowhere near their expectations.

Have you ever wondered why it is that Christ chose to appear to these women first after His resurrection? Was there something symbolic about it? I think the reason that these women were privileged to be the first witnesses of Christ's resurrection was because they were some of the few followers who didn't leave Jesus during His great trial. They were with Him at the cross when most of His disciples had deserted Him. They never left Jesus, even after His dead body was brought down from the cross and laid in the tomb. Mary Magdalene and the other Mary sat guard in front of the tomb for as long as they could without breaking the Sabbath.

Not only did these women never desert their Saviour, but they never stopped serving Him, even in death. Sacred Scripture tells us that, early in the morning, as early as they could possibly come without breaking the Sabbath, Mary Magdalene, Joanna, Mary the mother of James, and "other women" who followed Jesus out of Galilee, came with spices to anoint and prepare Jesus's body for burial.

This task of anointing the body was just another of the "woman's tasks" (like cooking, cleaning, washing, and sewing) that these women were accustomed to doing and, which I imagine, they had done for Jesus many times during His ministry. Because these women were taking care of Jesus's physical needs, they received one of the greatest privileges and blessings of all of our Lord's followers—to be the first witnesses of His resurrection. Christ acknowledged the faithful and loving service that these women had given Him throughout His mortal life. This acknowledgement emphasizes that what women do to sustain and provide physical life is valued in the eyes of God. Our Lord knew that these women's willingness to take care of His physical body, even after He was dead, was a sign of their tremendous love and devotion. And He blessed and rewarded them for it.

On that first Easter morning, the women who went to the tomb witnessed a history-changing event. And, they responded. In our lives, we too witness events, some of which shake our world. For example, most of us can remember exactly where we were and what we were doing on the morning of September 11, 2001, when a series of terrorist attacks were made by the Islamic terrorist group al-Qaeda on American soil. Or, the afternoon of November 22, 1963, when United States president, John F. Kennedy, was assassinated while riding in a motorcade in Dallas, Texas.

When we witness these events, for example, the terrorist attacks, how do we react? Do we react in the way the terrorists want us to—in fear? Or do we respond to the challenge with love and compassion for those most affected? The women at the tomb responded to their challenge with love. Do we do the same in the situations we witness?

Let us pray:

> Dear Lord,
> Thank You for directing my steps today.
> Thank You for covering me with Your protective veil.
> With You as my Guide, help me to know with confidence
> that no evil shall come near me, my family, my work, or my
> dwelling place.
>
> I rebuke all that is not of You for hindering my life
> and purpose.
> No storm, no demonic strategy, no offense, no pestilence,
> and no evil will interrupt your blessings in my life.
>
> Thank you, Father God, for the peace which passes
> all understanding.
>
> In Jesus's name, I pray.
> Amen.

Gender: Male

In about the year 1485, Italian Renaissance painter Sandro Botticelli created a panel painting titled *Venus and Mars*.[93] The painting depicts the Roman gods Venus, goddess of love, and Mars, god of war, in an allegory of beauty and valour. The youthful couple recline in a forest setting, surrounded by playful baby satyrs. Building on Botticelli's imagery, American author John Gray wrote the popular text titled *Men Are from Mars, Women Are from Venus*. Gray asserts

---

93   https://www.nationalgallery.org.uk/paintings/sandro-botticelli-venus-and-mars

that each gender can be understood in terms of the distinct ways in which they respond to particular situations.

With that in mind, and now that we have looked at the expression of religiosity by women, let's move to the expression of religiosity by men.

When I think about the expression of religiosity by men, my thoughts move to my favourite saint—Saint Joseph the Worker. Also known as St. Joseph the Silent, he is the patron saint of husbands and fathers, the patron saint of families, the patron saint of homes, and the patron saint of workers. St. Joseph is the patron and protector of the Catholic Church; as well as his patronages of the sick and of a happy death, due to the belief that he died in the presence of Jesus and Mary. Saint Joseph is my favourite saint because, in addition to being a husband, I have been blessed by God to be a father.

Speaking of fatherhood, I'll never forget the moment I held our first-born for the first time. Wendy was exhausted, I was excited like a child on Christmas morning waiting to unwrap that long awaited gift, and we were so very much in love. A part of me couldn't believe that the waiting was over. Our daughter, Rebecca, was in my arms.

Another part of me knew, with absolute certainty, that my life would never be the same. In one brief moment, after nine months of anticipation, "*a man changes into a father as he sets eyes on his child for the first time.*"[94] My friends, nothing in life will ever make you as happy, as sad, as exhausted, or as incredibly proud as fatherhood. In my life,

---

94   https://proudhappymama.com/45-new-dad-quotes-about-becoming-a-father-for-the-first-time/

of all the titles I've been privileged to have, "Dad" has always been the best.

Back to the account of St. Joseph. I have a small statue of St. Joseph with the child Jesus in my den, a reminder as I work at my table of the qualities of this great saint, the man who was closest to Jesus. Men, who are described as the strong, silent type, have a role model in St. Joseph. He was a man of few words, but his faith, his capacity to discern, his vigilance, his perseverance, his capacity to provide for and protect his family show St. Joseph as a strong and humble leader. If St. Joseph was with us today, people would know him as a quiet man, but when he spoke, his words would be profound. St. Joseph would be the go-to guy for great fatherly advice. His fidelity and his humility is a model for Christian men.

Sacred Scripture tells us little about St. Joseph's life. The Gospel according to St. Matthew goes to great length to record Joseph's lineage from King David and from Father Abraham. We do know that Joseph was a carpenter and that he lived in Nazareth. We also know that it was no coincidence that Joseph was engaged to be married to Mary. He was chosen by God for this special calling—to be the earthly father of Jesus.

I don't think any of us can imagine the flood of thoughts and emotions that must have filled Joseph's head and his heart when he received the news that he was chosen to raise and care for the Son of God, the promised Messiah, the Saviour of the world. "*Joseph's Song*"[95] by Michael Card does a pretty good job of capturing those thoughts and emotions. The lyrics go like this:

---

95   http://www.songlyrics.com/michael-card/joseph-s-song-lyrics/

How could it be this baby in my arms
sleeping now, so peacefully?
The Son of God, the angel said.
How could it be?

Lord, I know He's not my own
Not of my flesh, not of my bone.
Still Father let this baby be
the son of my love.

Father, show me where I fit into this plan of Yours
How can a man be father to the Son of God?
Lord, for all my life I've been a simple carpenter.
How can I raise a king, how can I raise a king?

He looks so small, His face and hands so fair
and when He cries the sun just seems to disappear.
But when He laughs, it shines again.
How could it be?

Father, show me where I fit into this plan of Yours
How can a man be father to the Son of God?
Lord, for all my life I've been a simple carpenter.
How can I raise a king, how can I raise a king?
How could it be this baby in my arms
sleeping now, so peacefully?
The Son of God, the angel said.
How could it be? How could it be?

We know that sometime after Jesus's birth in Bethlehem, the family returned to live in Nazareth. Only three other incidents are mentioned where Joseph was present. One was at the circumcision of

Jesus eight days after His birth (Luke 2:21–35) when they met Simeon who made prophecies about Jesus's future and spoke of a "*sword of sorrow*," which would pierce Mary's heart. Then, we read about an angel of the Lord speaking to Joseph in a dream about the need to take the child and His mother and flee to Egypt to avoid Herod's search for the child (Matthew 2:13–15). The final mention takes place when Jesus was 12 years old, and He went with Mary and Joseph to celebrate the Passover in Jerusalem (Luke 2:41–52).

Although we know little about Joseph's life, we know quite a bit about his character:

- **Joseph was righteous and merciful** (Matthew 1:19).

  Learning that his betrothed was with child, and being of the belief that Mary had been unfaithful to him, Joseph could easily have followed the Law of Moses by ending the engagement. Joseph chose, instead, to show righteousness and mercy. Although he set his mind on divorce, he decided to do it quietly and privately so that Mary would not be dishonoured or harmed.

- **Joseph trusted God** (Matthew 1:20–23).

  It took great faith to believe such an impossible story about Mary's pregnancy... the angel's statement that "*the child within her is from the Holy Spirit*." Even when there was no way to logically explain or understand the situation he faced, Joseph chose to trust God and step out in faith. Joseph could have "put Mary away" in disgrace when her pregnancy became obvious. But Joseph trusted what he had been told in a dream, and he stood by his wife-to-be.

- **Joseph was obedient** (Matthew 1:24).

Joseph demonstrated absolute obedience to God's call and commands. He obeyed God, taking Mary as his wife. The child's name would identify His mission. Jesus—derived from the Hebrew name Yeshua, which is based on the Semitic root meaning *"to deliver; to rescue."* As recorded in scripture, Joseph continued to be obedient to God's commands.

It was undoubtedly Joseph who negotiated a safe place for the birth of Jesus from a reluctant innkeeper. It was Joseph who responded to another dream, and led his family to safety as refugees from Herod's power-crazed murder of Bethlehem's children. It was Joseph who carefully shielded Jesus in Egypt, and then, when the time was right, settled his family in Nazareth.

The important, underlying emphasis of St. Matthew's narrative is the vital importance of Joseph's obedience: doing what God asked him to do. As the head of his brand-new family, it is Joseph's faithful obedience to God that saves and preserves Jesus for the ministry that is to come. Joseph does not do what we might expect a man in his position to do. He does not divorce his wife for shame. He does not ignore the messages he receives through his dreams. He doesn't act all macho and try to protect his son from Herod's soldiers with his own strength and cunning. No, he simply trusts and obeys what God tells him to do. He welcomes the newborn king, and then safely shields him from harm until the danger of Herod is past.

- **Joseph was devoted to and protective of his family** (Matthew 2:13–15; 19–23).

  With deep trust in God's providence, Joseph took Mary as his wife and accepted the child to whom she would give birth. It's been said the best thing a father can do for his children is to love their mother. Joseph demonstrated unconditional love for Mary with his undying devotion. He cared for Jesus as his own son and did what was necessary to keep both Jesus and His mother safe from danger. By accepting his role as earthly father to the Messiah, Joseph teaches us about faithful obedience to God's plan in our lives.

- **Joseph honoured God** (Luke 2:21–24; 41).

  Joseph followed all the religious customs according to the Law of Moses. As an observant Jew and a lover of the Law of God, Joseph made the long journey to the temple in Jerusalem each year for the great feasts. This was one way for him to demonstrate that his whole life was turned toward the God of Israel. With him went his beloved wife, Mary, and the child Jesus.

What I find to be particularly interesting is that nowhere in the Sacred Gospels do we ever hear anything that Joseph says. Joseph is not a man of words. He is a man of action. Joseph does what the angel tells him: he takes Mary as his wife; he goes to Bethlehem; he finds a place to stay for the night; he takes his family to safety in Egypt.

That's a huge list of responsibilities for a man of few words! But it is a perfect job for a man of action. St. Joseph appears in the Gospels as a strong and courageous man, a working man. We see in St. Joseph a man of great tenderness with a capacity for concern, compassion, a genuine openness to others, and love.

And just as God had a plan for Joseph, God has a plan for each one of us. The plan need not be an elaborate one. In its simplest form, God wants us to follow the law and observe the commandments. We may feel insignificant, that we have nothing to offer. Still, God has a plan for you. And, God has a plan for me.

In the everyday business of living, God actually leaves us alone most of the time. In sacred Scripture, God has already made it clear *how* we are to live our lives. He then gives humanity the free will to decide whether we will choose to live as we've been called. We are to love God and love our neighbours. Or, if you prefer a more poetic phrase, we have been instructed through the prophet Micah to *"do justice, love kindness and walk humbly with your God"* (Micah 6:8).

These were, in fact, the precise attitudes of Joseph. Doing justice meant that he could not "put away" a young woman whose unplanned pregnancy was not her fault. Loving mercy meant that he was to give her the protection she and her baby needed. Walking humbly with God meant trusting that God's plan for the baby was far superior to anything that Joseph himself might consider.

God can instantly change the planned direction of anyone's life, and He did just that with Joseph. Joseph probably thought his life was pretty well planned out with his marriage and vocation having been arranged neatly for him. But just when everything looked promising, his world came crashing down. He discovered that his bride-to-be was pregnant. Joseph was facing a dilemma that probably seemed hopeless.

All of us face troubling situations that require tough decisions. God allows us to go through difficult times we may not understand so that we can learn to place our trust in Him. It is never easy, but if we can learn to trust God even in those times of confusion and uncertainty, our faith will be strong no matter what might come our way. This was the case with Joseph. God was preparing him for a time when he would have to make decisions for his young family based entirely on faith and trust in God.

So, what about you? Are you going through a time of uncertainty with a difficult decision to make? Is God calling on you for something special? Maybe you need to ask yourself, "For what new adventure is God preparing me?" I invite you to consider whether the choice you have to make will extend God's kingdom of love, or get in the way. All I can do, with the full weight of scripture and God's story behind me, is invite you to carry on doing justly, loving mercy, and walking humbly with your God … just as Joseph did.

Let us pray:[96,97,98]

> St. Joseph, Guardian of the Redeemer,
> Spouse of the Blessed Virgin Mary.
> To you, God entrusted his only Son;

---

96   In the opening stanza of his apostolic letter on St. Joseph, Patris Corde, the Holy Father, Pope Francis says: "WITH A FATHER'S HEART: that is how Joseph loved Jesus, whom all four Gospels refer to as the son of Joseph". The greatness of Saint Joseph is that he was the spouse of Mary and the earthly father of Jesus. In this way, he placed himself, in the words of Saint John Chrysostom, "*at the service of the entire plan of salvation*". In a footnote to his apostolic letter, Pope Francis notes that for more than 40 years, he has said a special prayer to St. Joseph each day.

97   https://www.vatican.va/content/francesco/en/apost_letters/documents/papa-francesco-lettera-ap_20201208_patris-corde.html

98   https://psalm91.com/prayer-to-the-sleeping-saint-joseph/

in you, Mary placed her trust;
with you, Christ became man.

Blessed Joseph, who has power to render possible even things which are considered impossible, come to our aid. Take under your protection the troubling situations that I commend to you, that they may have a happy outcome.

Dear Saint Joseph, confident of the Lord's absolute power and goodness, look upon me. Take my need into your heart and present it to God's only Son. Help me then, good Saint Joseph, to hear the voice of God, to arise, and to act with love.

St. Joseph, guide us that we may be upright and righteous.

That we may be men and women after God's will.

That we may be able to pray with single-minded commitment, *"Dear Father in heaven, show me how I fit into this plan of yours."*

Saint Joseph, humble working man of Nazareth, man of so few words, pray for us!

Amen.

Personal Health Status and Functional Independence

There is an inverse relationship between health indicators and religious activities. That is, as health status and functional independence decline, religious behaviour increases. This is particularly reflective of unstructured activities such as private prayer, Bible reading, and tuning into religious programmes on radio and television.

Bell[99] identified that there was also a tendency for respondents, who had lower health status, to score higher on an internal sense of religiosity. Among older adults who either perceived their health to be poorer or were objectively rated as having declining health, private devotional activity tended to rate higher. Conversely, organized community-based religious activities were more frequent among older adults who reported and demonstrated better health status.

Levin and Markides[100] identified that the positive relationship between organizational activities such as church or synagogue attendance and personal adjustment or well-being may be complicated by the effects of physical health. Church attendance and level of involvement in other community activities, then, may simply be a proxy for good physical health.

Similarly, functional independence such as mobility is also a significant factor in attendance at formal services of worship.

When I think of personal health status and functional independence as factors in the practice of faith, I am reminded of Psalm 121. It goes like this:

I lift up my eyes to the hills—
from where will my help come?

99   Bell, W. C. (1989) Celebrate the harvest: A study of the spiritual needs of the older adult. M.H.A. University of Minnesota. Twin Cities Health Sciences (Bio-Medical) Library WT145 B435c 1989.

100 Levin, J.S. and Markides, K.S. (1986) Religious Attendance and Subjective Health. Journal for the Scientific Study of Religion.

My help comes from the LORD,
who made heaven and earth.

He will not let your foot be moved;
he who keeps you will not slumber.
He who keeps Israel
will neither slumber nor sleep.

The LORD is your keeper;
the LORD is your shade at your right hand.
The sun shall not strike you by day,
nor the moon by night.

The LORD will keep you from all evil;
he will keep your life.
The LORD will keep
your going out and your coming in
from this time on and forevermore.

Psalm 121 is one of the most well-known psalms in Judaism. Considered as a prayer for protection and trusting in God's providential care, Psalm 121 is one of 15 psalms referred to as *psalms of ascent*. There are differing scholarly opinions regarding the purpose for which this series of psalms were written. The most widely accepted opinion is that they were written as encouragement for the Jewish faithful going up to the House of the Lord in Jerusalem during the pilgrim festivals of Passover, Pentecost, and the Feast of Tabernacles.

My family has had the blessing of being able to visit the Holy Land on a couple of occasions, so we know firsthand that Jerusalem is situated at a high elevation compared to everything around it. Mount

Zion, the heart and high point of the Old City in Jerusalem, is about 770 meters (2,550 feet) above sea level. Irrespective of which direction you go once you get outside the Jerusalem metropolitan area, it's basically downhill. If you travel southeast, past the Mount of Olives, you will be moving downhill all the way to the Dead Sea. From the Temple Mount to the Dead Sea is only 23 kilometres (14 miles) as the crow flies, but the drop in elevation is almost 1,220 metres (4,000 feet). Jericho, to the northeast of Jerusalem, is the same straight-line distance (about 23 kilometres) from Jerusalem. But from the Temple Mount to Jericho is a 1,036-metre (3,400-foot) drop in elevation.

Those changes in elevation are extreme, even for the seasoned foot traveller. To make matters worse, when you travel that climb from Jericho to Jerusalem, the route will take you on a precarious roadway that weaves around the edges of a steep canyon for about 35 kilometres (22 miles). It's a dangerous ascent, but that was the route taken by thousands of pilgrims as they travelled from Galilee to Judea for the great feast days.

As travellers made their way up that treacherous road, they would sing these psalms. That, most commentators agree, is why these are called *psalms of ascent*. So, these are songs for pilgrims.

As the psalmist looks toward the mountains, he understands the dangers he could meet along the way. The travellers to Jerusalem faced many dangers on their journey. Sunstroke was a real concern during the day, and there were often extreme changes of temperature between day and night. The moon was associated with lunacy. And, of course, there was also the danger of bandits and wild animals at night. There were dangers both day and night on the road, but verse six assured the traveller: "*The sun will not strike you by day, nor the moon by night.*"

Psalm 121 is a celebration of security for people in very insecure circumstances. Every verse is full of comfort and confidence. It's one of those totally triumphant, joyously upbeat passages of scripture given to us as reminders that our heavenly Father is ever present. We can rest secure in His loving kindness, even when we are surrounded by deadly dangers of all kinds. It is a psalm that should encourage you in every imaginable trial, tragedy, or calamity of life.

But do not be fooled, my friends. The comforts and guarantees in this psalm are not merely temporal reassurances for earthbound pilgrims on the ascent to Jerusalem. Rather, these are heavenly promises of spiritual blessings for each and every one of us as we make our pilgrimage to the Heavenly Jerusalem. You'll find proof that this eternal perspective is the key to understanding Psalm 121 if you pay heed to the last word of the last line: "*The LORD will keep your going out and your coming in from this time on and **forevermore**.*"

Keep that eternal perspective in mind. You'll miss the true significance of Psalm 121 if you think only in terms of earthly security on a 35-kilometre journey up a mountain road. The scope of this psalm is infinitely larger than that. It's not so much about physical safety and bodily protection—it's about the eternal preservation of our souls and the unshakable security of our spiritual standing before God. The psalmist is simply using the theme of journeying mercies to illustrate the benefits and blessings of God's inexhaustible mercy to those who trust Him.

Let us pray:

> Loving Saviour,
>
> In my times of deep distress and suffering, thank You for bringing others to walk alongside me, through the different seasons of my life, to comfort and encourage, to help and advise.
>
> Thank You for all those whom You have used to draw near to me to be Your hands to help, Your arms to support, and Your heart to love.
>
> In the same way that You have sent others to accompany me during the troubled times in my life, I pray, Lord Jesus, send me to be a vessel of comfort for others who are facing similar difficulties and are themselves in need of comfort and help.
>
> Send me, I pray. Send me.
>
> I ask this in Your most holy name.
>
> Amen.

Spousal Health Status and Functional Independence

Having a spouse who is ill or disabled can be a major source of distress, particularly when active caregiving support is required from their partner. The literature suggests that the detrimental effects of caregiving are primarily due to the patient's functional disabilities and behavioural problems, and the associated care demands.

However, distress or depression in one spouse can lead to depression in their partner, even in the absence of illness and disability that require caregiving. The common thread linking these realities is that both involve exposure to the suffering of an intimate partner. The fact is that exposure to suffering is a unique and powerful stressor that affects the physical and psychological well-being of those who are exposed to it.

In 2010, the *American Journal of Geriatric Psychiatry* (AJGP) reported on a study that sought to examine whether the suffering of an older adult may uniquely and independently contribute to depression and cardiovascular disease (CVD) in their spouse.[101] Suffering was defined as "*a state of distress associated with events that threaten the integrity of an individual as a complex physical, social, psychological, and spiritual being.*"[102] Ferrell and Coyle[103] identified that suffering includes such qualities as multidimensional distress/pain/discomfort, loss of control, helplessness, inability to cope, anxiety, and depression. Taken together, the literature suggests that there are three measurable universal manifestations of suffering. They include:

1. physical symptoms such as chronic or acute pain, nausea, and dyspnea;

2. psychological symptoms of distress, such as depression and anxiety; and

---

101 Richard Schulz, R. Beach, & Scott, et al. (2009). Spousal suffering and partner's depression and cardiovascular disease: The cardiovascular health study. *American Journal of Geriatric Psychiatry, 17*(3), 246–254.

102 Cassell, E. J. (2004). *The nature of suffering and the goals of medicine.* Oxford University Press.

103 Ferrell, B. R., & Coyle N. (2008). The nature of suffering and the goals of nursing. *Oncology Nursing Forum, 35,* 241–247.

3. indicators of existential/spiritual well-being, which include measures of inner harmony, meaning and purpose of life, and the extent to which individuals find comfort and strength in religious beliefs.

The AJGP study reported on a dose–response relationship between suffering in a spouse and concurrent depression in their partner, as well as a relationship between suffering and the partner's future risk for depression. Husbands exposed to wives reporting high levels of suffering also had higher rates of prevalent cardio-vascular disease (CVD). Kroenke et al. suggest that the fact that similar physical health effects were not found among wives could be due to the generally lower levels of CVD among women, husbands' lower rates of suffering, and/or reluctance among males to express symptoms of suffering as compared to females.[104]

Obviously, there are limitations to this observational work, so the reader should be cautious in making causal inferences about relationships between a patient's suffering and their loved one's depression and CVD.

Spirituality has been shown to buffer the adverse effects of stress, but few studies have examined the role of spirituality on the relationship between caregiving stress and spousal caregivers' mental and physical health. Colgrove et al.[105] found that caregiver stress was less prominent among caregivers who demonstrated a high level of spirituality. In other words, spirituality had a stress-buffering effect. That

---

104 Kroenke K., & Spitzer R. L. (1998). Gender difference in the reporting of physical and somatoform symptoms. *Psychosom Med.*, 60, 150–155.

105 Colgrove, L., Youngmee, K., & Thompson, N. (2007). The effect of spirituality on the quality of life of spousal caregivers of cancer survivors. *Annals of behavioural medicine: A publication of the society of behavioural medicine*, 33, 90–98.

is, the findings suggest that maintaining faith and finding meaning in caregiving tend to buffer the adverse effect of caregiving stress on mental health.

Spousal health status and functional independence are factors which impact one's participation in community-based religious activities. As one's spouse's health status declines, one's ability to participate in activities outside of the home also declines. This is particularly so when there is a caregiver role required for the spouse whose health status or functional independence is declining. This is not to suggest that spousal health status is a deterrent to personal expression of faith in other non-organizational activities such as private prayer, Bible reading, and tuning into religious programmes on radio and television.

When I think about the influence that spousal health status tends to have on active participation in community-based and non-organizational religious activities, I am reminded of a passage from the Book of Ecclesiastes, which says:

> Two are better than one, because they have a good reward for their toil. For if they fall, one will lift up the other; but woe to one who is alone and falls and does not have another to help. Again, if two lie together, they keep warm; but how can one keep warm alone? And though one might prevail against another, two will withstand one. A threefold cord is not quickly broken (Ecclesiastes 4:9–12).

The writer's picture of relationship is of two intertwined strands of rope, each with their own individuality and limitations, but they are better when joined and working together. If they pull in opposite directions, that is different, of course! However, if they wrap themselves around each other through their union, they form something stronger than two individual strands, for they give strength to each other through their union.

"A threefold cord is not quickly broken." This is scientifically accurate. Three intertwined strands—no more, no less—is the strongest kind of rope. Two strands alone are unstable because they can easily unravel under pressure and slide over each other with friction. But the third strand fixes the other two into place and adds its strength to them such that three intertwined strands are bound firmly together. So, who is this third strand, who will make all the difference?

Of course, it is God Himself. He has revealed His inner nature as being three persons (Father, Son, and Spirit) intertwined together in one and bound together in unity in perfect love, just like a rope of three strands. This is a picture of the Trinity and, in a God-centred marriage, we come the closest to fulfilling His call to be His image here on Earth.

Using imagery from our natural world, I want to focus your attention now on a gaggle of migrating Canada geese.[106] I am sure most of you have noticed that Canada geese fly in a "V" formation. It is an amazing thing to see a flock of geese flying across the sky in their formation, honking as they fly. As each goose flaps its wings, it creates an air lift for those geese flying behind. In fact, this allows the entire group to fly 71% farther than if they were flying alone.

If a goose is not paying attention and falls out of formation, it suddenly feels the drag and resistance of flying alone. It quickly moves

---

106 Adapted from https://ccednet-rcdec.ca/en/story-of-the-goose

back into formation to take advantage of the lifting power of the bird immediately in front of it.

When the lead goose tires, it rotates back into the formation, and another goose flies to the point position to lead the group. The geese flying in formation honk to encourage those up front to keep up their speed.

When a goose gets sick, wounded, or is shot down, two geese drop out of formation and follow it down to the ground to protect it. They stay with the weakened goose until it dies or recovers sufficiently to be able to fly again. Then, they launch out with another formation, or catch up with the flock. If they can't find their original group, they are welcomed to join any other gaggle that comes along.

Supporting each other and working together allows Canada geese to travel between 630 and 800 kilometres (400 to 500 miles), averaging about 90 kilometres per hour (55 miles per hour) for 12 hours a day, to get to warmer climates for the winter.

Why have I been talking about Canada geese? Because healthy, spirit-filled interdependent relationships are like those Canada geese. Like a community, people working together to support each other. Like a marriage, living it on a day-by-day, experience-by-experience basis.

How is marriage like a flock of migrating Canada geese?

- People who share a common direction and sense of community can get where they are going quicker and easier because they are travelling on the thrust of one another. A marriage is like that where husband and wife care about each other, are a community, and support and encourage each other in their life journey.

- Geese stay in formation with those headed where they want to go. A marriage is like that where husband and wife are willing to accept each other's help and give help to one another.

- Geese take turns doing the hard tasks and sharing leadership. Leading the gaggle is a difficult and tiring job for the leader. So, when tired, the leader drops back into the group and another goose takes the lead. Each one is dependent on the one in front. A marriage is like that where husband and wife are dependent on each other's skills, capabilities, and unique arrangements of gifts, talents, and resources.

- Geese honk as they fly, encouraging those in front to keep up the speed. A marriage is like that where husband and wife encourage one another to build a better and more loving community. Caring for the other when he or she is in pain or suffering is part of that encouragement.

- Geese stand by each other in difficult times, never abandoning a member until death. Canada geese mate for life, never abandoning their mate until death, and each member of the gaggle supports every other member. A marriage is like that where husband and wife are fully engaged in the other's life every step of the journey.

Let us pray:

My Jesus,

As we come before You today, we place our marriage in Your gentle hands.

Search our hearts, Lord. Convict us and clear out anything in our relationship that is not of You. Restore our right relationship with You, so that You, and You alone, are at the centre of our lives. Remind us that You are the third strand that binds us together through good times and tough times.

Father God, give us the strength to be brave. Replace with Christ-centred courage, the fear of what might happen and what the future might hold.

Holy Spirit, empower us with humility, gentleness, patience, peace, and unity. Curb our frustration and our inadequacy from morphing into bitterness and distress. Forgive us for the times when we lose our patience with one another.

O Lord, help all married couples with an abundance of Your grace so that they may better symbolize the mystery of Your Church.

Be with us, we pray.

Amen.

Death of a Spouse

Death of a spouse at any age is a life-shattering experience. For older adults, bereavement can have a particularly devastating effect on their immune system and cause them to lose interest in their own care. For some, the death of a loved one can result in stress cardiomyopathy, often referred to as broken heart syndrome. This may in part explain why many seniors experience a severe decline in health, or even pass away, shortly after the loss of a spouse. The risk of an older person dying within the first three months following the death of their spouse is greatly increased.[107]

Widowhood/widowerhood is among the most stressful of all life events and requires more psychological and behavioural adjustment than any other life transition.[108] Because older adults have solidified and internalized a lifetime of habits, behaviours, and attitudes, the behavioural adjustments associated with late-life bereavement may be one of the most difficult challenges an older adult will face.

Couples who are frail or ill may have been able to maintain their independence together by compensating for one another. For example, a wife with limited mobility may have relied on her husband to help her get up and down the stairs, or carry items such as groceries. She, in return, may have been covering for his memory loss by prompting him to take his medication, pay bills, or providing directions in the car. In these cases, when an older person loses their spouse, their

---

107 https://www.merckmanuals.com/professional/geriatrics/social-issues-in-older-adults/effects-of-life-transitions-on-older-adults

108 Thompson L. W., Breckenridge J. N., Gallagher D., & Peterson J. (1984). Effects of bereavement on self-perceptions of physical health in elderly widows and widowers. *Journal of Gerontology,* 39, 309–314.

inability to manage daily tasks on their own becomes apparent and they are no longer able to manage on their own.

Even for those seniors who are in good health, there will be many new and overwhelming tasks to learn. Many older couples have set roles within their marriage, where one spouse is solely responsible for a certain job. For example, many husbands have never been required to prepare a meal or wash their clothes and consequently may struggle with domestic chores. Or, if the responsibility of paying bills and managing funds fell to her husband, a widow may feel at a loss when faced with financial decisions. Having to acquire these new skills during a period of grief can seem insurmountable.

Seniors who suffer the loss of a spouse can feel plunged into isolation. If they were living independently, as opposed to congregate housing, the surviving spouse is now alone. Often, older couples are always together and therefore don't feel the need to develop a wider social network. In those cases, the loss of their lifelong companion is felt in every aspect of their day, not to mention having to sleep alone, often for the first time in decades. Meals, routines, and outings such as afternoon walks may get neglected, causing the surviving spouse to get stuck in a downward spiral of loneliness and depression.

Upon widowhood/widowerhood, the survivor must relinquish the status of married person and assume the identity of widow or widower. In response to this identity transition, bereaved persons may realign their social networks or alter their social activities. In the absence of a significant other, social interactions outside of the marital relationship may become increasingly important, thereby increasing the bereaved person's level of social involvement. Alternatively, social relationships may become strained if the widow/

widower feels like a "fifth wheel" among married friends, thereby decreasing the bereaved person's level of social engagement.

Relationships with old friends change markedly in widowhood/widowerhood. Widows and widowers tend to look to their offspring for companionship, emotional support, and selected support assistance rather than seeking social support from new acquaintances. The reality is that, while most seniors gradually adapt to life without their spouse, they face many challenges.

Current literature suggests that marital status is a factor in the personal expression of faith. The assumption is that women often serve as the primary social contact and, thereby, the link to the social and spiritual community for their spouses. Hence, widowerhood status can be said to affect the community-based religious practice of males more than females.

When I think about widowhood and navigating difficult circumstances, my thoughts turn to the biblical account of the lives of Ruth and Naomi in the Book of Ruth. There was a great famine in Israel during the time when the judges ruled. Many Israelites relocated to foreign lands in order to feed their families. A man from Bethlehem named Elimelek took his wife, Naomi, and their two sons, Mahlon and Kilion, to Moab in search of a better life.

Now, for those of you who know your biblical history, you will recall that it was in Moab where God renewed His covenant with the Israelites before they entered the Promised Land (Deuteronomy 29). Moses died there (Deuteronomy 34:5–8), prevented by God from entering the Promised Land. He was buried in an unknown location in Moab and the Israelites spent a period of thirty days there in mourning.

Back to the story of Ruth and Naomi. While in Moab, Elimelek died and Naomi continued to live with her two sons, who had married Moabite women, Orpah and Ruth. After some time, both sons also passed away, leaving Naomi with her two foreign daughters-in-law.

Marooned in Moab, Naomi decides to return to her home in Bethlehem. One of her foreign daughters-in-law, Ruth, though a Moabite herself, insists that she join Naomi for the journey. We read Ruth's refusal to turn away from her mother-in-law, saying:

> "*Do not press me to leave you or to turn back from following you! Where you go, I will go; where you lodge, I will lodge; your people shall be my people, and your God my God. Where you die, I will die... there will I be buried. May the Lord do thus and so to me, and more as well, if even death parts me from you!*"
> (Ruth 1:16–17).

Naomi relents and begrudgingly allows Ruth to accompany her to Israel.

As is the case with many women featured in sacred Scripture, we are not provided with a lot of details about Naomi. We do know her name meant "sweet" or "pleasant," and after she loses all the male relatives in her immediate family, she changes her name to mean "bitter." Name changes in the ancient world were significant, for it signalled a substantial change in a person's character or life circumstances. An example is St. Paul who, after his conversion, was determined to bring the Gospel to the Gentiles. He dusted off his Jewsih name, Saul, and became known as Paul, a name to which Gentiles were accustomed. Or Abraham, whose name God changed from Abram. Or Simon, whose name was changed to Cephas (Peter). We read in the Holy Gospel according to St. Matthew:

> *And Jesus answered him, "Blessed are you, Simon son of Jonah! For flesh and blood has not revealed this to you, but my Father in heaven. And I tell you, you are Peter, and on this rock, I will build my church, and the gates of Hades will not prevail against it. I will give you the keys of the kingdom of heaven, and whatever you bind on earth will be bound in heaven, and whatever you loose on earth will be loosed in heaven"*
> (Matthew 16:17–19).

Back to the story: Naomi, now widowed and with no hope for a future, gives herself a new identity of bitterness. She places the blame on God, whom she accuses of having dealt with her harshly (Ruth 1:20–21). Nevertheless, God's plan continues to unfold. He provides Ruth with Boaz, a kinsman-redeemer, who helps the two widows, Naomi and Ruth, in their destitute circumstances. As time moves onward, Ruth marries Boaz. They have a son named Obed and a grandson named Jesse who would be the father of David and from whose genealogy would come the Messiah, our Lord and Saviour Jesus Christ. Naomi was saddened and embittered by her life circumstances, but in the end, Naomi is blessed in her old age.

There are several life lessons that we can learn from Naomi, particularly when it comes to perseverance in the face of difficult circumstances. Bolinger[109] offers three particular life lessons, as follows:

1. **God Continues to Move Amid Life's Hardships**

   Like Naomi, it is not unusual to feel abandoned by God when tragedy strikes our lives. Naomi by no means had an easy go of things. In a foreign land, she loses her husband and her two sons. She returns to her hometown with no prospects and very little means to survive. As she journeys forth, God continues to work in her life. By Naomi opening her heart and life to Ruth, permitting her to come along to Bethlehem and work in the fields, Ruth met Boaz. And this blessing redeemed both women. In the end, Naomi gains a son-in-law, and through her line, the Saviour of the world redeems mankind.

   God continues to work in our lives, too, when tragedy strikes.

2. **We Can Help Others in Our Difficult Moments**

   At first glance, we may think that Naomi does absolutely nothing in the story. She despairs when her family passes away, but it is Ruth who works in the fields to provide for both of them.

   Keep in mind Naomi was not a young woman. Grief had paralyzed her. Even before the two of them come to Bethlehem, she tries to send her daughters-in-law away from her to find new husbands. After all, she doesn't want them tied down to having to help an old woman. Nevertheless, as soon as Naomi learns about Boaz, she praises the Lord because she wants

---

109 Sourced from an article by Hope Bolinger at https://www.crosswalk.com/faith/bible-study/encouraging-truths-from-naomi-life-in-the-bible.html

Ruth to have a good home and a husband. Throughout the narrative, it is obvious that Naomi is looking out for Ruth, even in the midst of paralyzing grief.

3. **God Redeems the Broken-hearted**

   Naomi thought her family line had ended, but God continues it through Boaz and Ruth. Naomi gains a son-in-law and a family. There are other examples in sacred Scripture of people who think they will have no offspring. As one example, Abraham and Sarah didn't have their first child until Sarah was well past her childbearing years.

The story of Ruth reminds us that even when we think that we've come face-to-face with a brick wall and can't see how anything good can possibly come out of our circumstances, God is rooting for us. We read in the Book of the Prophet Jeremiah:

> *For surely, I know the plans I have for you, says the Lord, plans for your welfare and not for harm, to give you a future with hope. Then when you call upon me and come and pray to me, I will hear you. When you search for me, you will find me; if you seek me with all your heart…* (Jeremiah 29:11–13).

When a parent, spouse, relative, or friend passes away, he or she leaves a void that cannot be filled. We feel their absence acutely, yet as time goes on, the pain of our grief begins to fade. In the Jewish faith, reciting Mourning Prayers (Kaddish) for a relative that has died provides a tangible way to reinforce the connection we had in this life.

The English translation of Kaddish[110] follows:

> *Glorified and sanctified be God's great name through-out the world which He has created according to His will. May He establish His kingdom in your lifetime and during your days, and within the life of the entire House of Israel, speedily and soon; and say, Amen.*
>
> *May His great name be blessed forever and to all eternity.*
>
> *Blessed and praised, glorified and exalted, extolled and honored, adored and lauded be the name of the Holy One, blessed be He, beyond all the blessings and hymns, praises and consolations that are ever spoken in the world; and say, Amen.*
>
> *May there be abundant peace from heaven, and life, for us and for all Israel; and say, Amen.*
>
> *He who creates peace in His celestial heights, may He create peace for us and for all Israel; and say, Amen.*

Although Jewish law requires that Kaddish be recited following the death of a loved one, it is noteworthy that there is no reference—not a single word—about death in the prayer. This is because the theme of Kaddish is not about death. Rather, Kaddish is about the great-ness of God, who conducts the entire universe. Kaddish is a prayer for peace from the only One who can guarantee it—peace between

---

110 Adapted from https://www.jcam.org/Prayer.pdf

nations, peace between individuals, and peace of mind. Kaddish reminds us that with the passing of the beloved individual, his or her soul now rests with the One who brought it into being in the first place.

Significance of Religious Experience in One's Younger Years

For young adults and older adults alike, a religious family focus or upbringing is related to religious practice as an adult.[111] Early ideas from the family of origin influence religious beliefs in adulthood. Young adults, particularly those in their teenage years, often seem to rebel, choosing to challenge old beliefs and explore new ideas. Nevertheless, religious beliefs appear to be related to childhood upbringing. Similarly, for older adults, religious beliefs in early family life may have lasting effects, even later in life.[112]

Some research findings go so far as to suggest that religiosity in older adulthood can, in fact, be predicted by one's experiences as a young child being raised in a religious (or a nonreligious) family environment. Does this suggest stability in religiosity across adulthood? Remember, older adults have higher levels of religious commitment and participation than any other age group.[113]

---

111 Seifert, L. S. (2002). Toward a psychology of religion, spirituality, meaning-search, and aging: Past research and a practical application. *Journal of Adult Development, 9*, 61–70.

112 Wink, P. & Dillon, M. (2002). Spiritual development across the adult life course: Findings from a longitudinal study. *Journal of Adult Development. 9*, 79–94.

113 McFadden, S. H. (1996). Religion, spirituality, and aging. In J. E. Birren & K. Warner Schaie (eds.). *Handbook of the psychology of aging* (4th ed.). pp. 162–177. Academic Press.

In short, it appears that the life circumstances of older adulthood tend to cause the person to draw upon his or her religious upbringing as a child. Our life circumstances as older adults may cause us to return to that which was familiar, to bring into play a positive source of comfort learned at a previous time in our lives.

When I think about scriptural examples related to the significance of religious upbringing and its effects into adulthood, I am reminded of the Book of Daniel. The Biblical account of Daniel the prophet begins in approximately 604 BC. As children, Daniel and his friends had a Jewish upbringing. Daniel's parents chose a Hebrew name for their son, the name meaning "God is my judge," testifying to their faith in the one true God. When Daniel was a young man, around 13 or 14 years of age, Jerusalem was besieged by King Nebuchadnezzar of Babylon. The city and the Temple were destroyed. Many of Israel's finest citizens were taken captive and carried off to Babylon. Among those deported to Babylon were four young men from the tribe of Judah: Daniel and his friends Hananiah, Azariah, and Mishael.

Once in captivity, the youths were given new names. Daniel was named Belteshazzar, Hananiah was named Shadrach, Mishael was named Meshach, and Azariah was named Abednego. These four Babylonian names seem to refer to some of the false gods worshipped by the Babylonians.

Before entering the king's service, the young men were subjected to an intense re-education process during which time they were taught the language, literature, and culture of the Babylonians. Every possible effort was made to make them forget the God of their people and to embrace Babylon's pagan culture. But, despite the constant pressure to subvert their faith, Daniel, Hananiah, Azariah, and Mishael remained true to Jehovah throughout their years in Babylon.

These four Hebrew youths soon proved themselves to be exceptionally wise. As a result, they found favour with King Nebuchadnezzar. When Daniel turned out to be the only man capable of interpreting one of Nebuchadnezzar's troubling dreams, the king placed him in a high position over the whole province of Babylon, including over all the wise men of the land. At Daniel's request, the king appointed Shadrach, Meshach, and Abednego as Daniel's advisors.

As foretold through the prophet Jeremiah (Jeremiah 25:11), the Babylonian captivity of Judah's citizens lasted for 70 years. During this time, Daniel served in prominent positions in the governments of several Babylonian and Medo-Persian rulers, including Nebuchadnezzar, Belshazzar, Darius, and, finally, Cyrus. The Book of Daniel speaks of the challenges which these young men faced, including the deliverance of Shadrach, Meshach, and Abednego from the fiery furnace after their refusal to worship King Nebuchadnezzar's golden image (Daniel 3:8-25); the handwriting on the wall (Daniel 5) that spelled out the defeat of Belshazzar at the hands of the Medes and the Persians; and Daniel's culminating experience in the lion's den (Daniel 6).

You may have seen drawings of Daniel as a strapping young man looking peaceful amid pacing, ravenous lions. The reality is that Daniel is estimated to have been in his early eighties when this event happened. He was also, by that point, so respected that King Cyrus was planning to acclaim Daniel as overseer of the entire kingdom.

Sentenced to death for praying publicly to God as he had every day of his life, every effort was made to get Daniel to compromise. But compromise he would not. Bravely, the now elderly man chose courage over cowardice. After spending an entire night in an underground pit filled with hungry lions (that were expected to eat him alive), Daniel was released the next morning, unharmed. Protected by God, Daniel "*was found blameless before him*" (Daniel 6:22). No one seemed happier than the remorseful King Cyrus when he rushed to the mouth of the lions' den at dawn and discovered that Daniel was alive and unscathed.

Shortly after this event, King Cyrus allowed the Jewish people, whom Nebuchadnezzar had brought to Babylon in captivity, to return home to Jerusalem, instructing them to rebuild the Jerusalem Temple, which Nebuchadnezzar had destroyed. Cyrus also returned more than 5,000 priceless articles, including gold and silver dishes, pans, and bowls, that Nebuchadnezzar had stolen from the temple some 70 years earlier. King Cyrus financed the journey, and gave the returning Judeans whatever they needed, including bulls, rams, and lambs for burnt offerings, as well as wheat, oil, and wine to sustain them (Ezra 1:1–4). In essence, King Cyrus did everything he could to undo the destruction that had been wrought upon the Temple by Nebuchadnezzar.

The Book of Daniel is a grand tribute to the providence of God and His lordship of history and the universe. From the time Daniel arrived in Babylon, the pressure was on to indoctrinate him into the Babylonian culture. And yet despite the incredible day-by-day, hour-by-hour social and political pressure to convert, throughout their lifetime in captivity, Daniel and his three friends stayed true to the faith of their fathers. True to the faith which they had learned as children in Judea. They lived, worked, and even thrived in a pagan culture, without letting it undermine their relationship with the God of Israel.

It is not unlike how we are challenged to respond at times in today's modern and increasingly secular world. It is not unlike how we are called to stand firm in support of Holy Mother Church's teachings when it comes to how the world around us would have us respond to issues such as abortion, assisted suicide, LGBTQ, and the list goes on.

Let us pray:

> St. Jude,[114] glorious apostle and martyr, patron saint of desperate cases, you are a faithful friend to all who rely on your intercession. Gracious patron and helper in time of adversity, I come to seek your help.
>
> The cross that I carry seems too heavy for me to bear; I feel anxious and discouraged in the face of this difficulty.
>
> Intercede for me that I may once again know the power of the Lord's redeeming love and the shield of His comfort in my life.
>
> Teach me, gracious patron, how to live by faith in Jesus's promise that He is with me always.
>
> Teach me to live in hope, relying on the Lord's saving power to bring me through this time of pain and suffering.

---

114 Adapted from https://yenra.com/catholic/prayers/share-a-prayer/archive094/

Teach me to live in love that I may be a light in the darkness for others.

Glory to the Father and to the Son and to the Holy Spirit as it was in the beginning,
is now, and ever shall be, world without end.

Amen.

Community Involvement

When I was in the midst of fighting to regain control over my body and to rid it of the invasive cancers, I regularly received phone calls, text messages, emails, and get-well cards from parishioners in the community where I served as a deacon. They truly cared about my welfare, and they lifted me up whenever possible through their prayers and their words of encouragement. In addition to my family, my church community was truly a rock during the storm. In my world, the community was involved.

Involvement need not be face-to-face. As we continue to journey with the COVID-19 pandemic, we have learned (if we didn't know before) that, given our world's tremendous communications technology, when we are physically prevented from sharing space with one another, we can worship in community even without being physically "in community."

Researchers have long known about the personal benefits of "social capital," the ties that build trust, connection, and participation. But this link may be particularly important for seniors, precisely because both our health and our social capital tend to decline as we age. We retire from jobs, lose friends and spouses to death, and see family members move to far-away places. These losses can sharply reduce daily social contacts and stimulation, which in turn have a direct impact on our health—social, spiritual, mental, and physical. Higher levels of social interaction, even peripheral interactions, can have a high payoff for older adults.

Older adults' level of religious participation is greater than that in any other age group. For older people, the religious community is the largest source of social support outside of the family. And, involvement in religious organizations is the most common type of voluntary social activity, more common than all other forms of voluntary social activity combined.

The idea of community comes from the sense of responsibility we have for each other. In sacred Scripture, God encourages us to take care of our brothers and sisters while following the Word of the Lord. Repeatedly throughout the Old Testament, we read God's commands to care for the widow, the orphan, and the foreigner. When He gave the Law to Moses and the Israelites, God gave clear instructions for how to treat those less fortunate among them, with harsh consequences promised if they failed in their responsibility (Exodus 22). Similarly, in the New Testament, James says that taking care of the needs of orphans and widows is part of religion "*unstained by the world*" (James 1:27). Caring for those in distress is not optional for followers of Christ.

In considering what our own attitude should be toward those less fortunate, it's helpful to remember that each one of us was adopted into God's family through Jesus Christ (Ephesians 1:3–7). It is our joy and our privilege to partner with God in loving, serving, and protecting those among us who are in need.

One does not have to look far to find examples in sacred Scripture of being involved in community. The Acts of the Apostles tells us:

> *They devoted themselves to the apostles' teaching and fellowship, to the breaking of bread and the prayers. Awe came upon everyone, because many wonders and signs were being done by the apostles. All who believed were together and had all things in common; they would sell their possessions and goods and distribute the proceeds to all, as any had need. Day by day, as they spent much time together in the temple, they broke bread at home and ate their food with glad and generous hearts, praising God and having the goodwill of all the people. And day by day the Lord added to their number those who were being saved* (Acts 2:42–47).

There is an African proverb which says, "*It takes a village to raise a child.*" That proverb reflects the emphasis, which African cultures place on family and community. I would suggest that the same phraseology can be used in referring to faith communities. They are, after all, "villages," or communities made up of like-minded believers.

Like those first apostles, the village, or community, of believers has been described as one in which believers connect with each other on a soul level and in so doing, spur each other on to a deeper relationship with God.[115] A faith community is more than just individual friendships. It is an atmosphere of deeply interconnected relationships. It can be likened

---

115 https://www.cru.org/us/en/train-and-grow/help-others-grow/discipleship/the-role-of-community-in-discipleship.html

to a home with an open door where your presence matters, where truth goes forth with grace, and where friends together pursue Christlikeness. Above all else, a home is a warm, inviting environment. In a home, you eat real food. In a home, everyone knows your name, someone takes your coat, and asks how your day has been. In a home, those present truly care about you.

In a village of believers, one finds members of all kinds, some mature and some young, some mentors and some peers. It is a place where the lost are welcome to join. The village helps make disciples by bringing God's Word alive in the context of community.

For several years, my wife and I were members of a Catholic sponsored evangelization initiative known as a "Live-In" whose sole purpose is to lead retreatants to a deeper personal relationship with Jesus Christ. A Live-In is a weekend retreat with the theme of "Getting to Know Jesus."[116] The weekend involves a series of talks and discussions pertaining to the Christian life. There are a variety of speakers from various walks of life. The entire program is instructive, uplifting, and enjoyable, with a variety of great activities. Being ecumenical in nature, participants experience worship from a variety of Christian traditions, including a Catholic Mass.

The Live-In movement in both Canada and St. Lucia is centred on our total and utter dependency on the grace of God. Consequently, the preparation leading up to, and the work at the Live-In itself, is immersed in and surrounded by prayer.

The Live-In movement is an excellent example of a village of likeminded believers focused on growing together in faith. I was blessed

---

116   http://www.reddeerlivein.com/

with serving on the movement's Edmonton-Strathcona leadership team and in the capacity of that team's overall director for a number of years. For me, the Live-In movement was a life-changing experience, which would later see me ordained into Holy Mother Church's Sacred Order of the Diaconate.

The Live-In movement was, and continues to be, all about developing a personal relationship with our Lord and Saviour, Jesus Christ. In ancient Israel, Jesus demonstrated the value of interconnectedness with His disciples. Seldom did Jesus spend time with just one disciple. He spent significant time with the multitudes, with the twelve, with three, or even by Himself to pray and be with the Father. Even in Jesus's most significant moments, such as the Transfiguration on Mount Tabor and in the Garden of Gethsemane, Jesus brought with Him not one, but several disciples.

This was the model of interconnectedness that the apostles brought into the early church. At Pentecost, *"those who welcomed his message were baptized, and that day about three thousand persons were added"* (Acts 2:41). Now one thing is clear: with 3,000 new believers, the apostles could not have individually met with each person on a regular basis. Very few ministries today could accommodate such rapid growth.

So, how did they do it? The story in Acts provides a few clues. *"They devoted themselves to the apostles' teaching and fellowship, to the breaking of bread and to prayers"* (Acts 2:42). Few, if any, buildings in ancient Jerusalem could have accommodated 3,000 people. No structure could accommodate such supernatural growth. Only a village of authentic believers could disciple the early church.

These new believers spent time together in smaller communities. The apostles travelled from house to house, from community to community, teaching the Word. The close-knit fellowship of the various communities contributed greatly to the growth of new believers, for we read, "*Awe came upon everyone, because many wonders and signs were being done by the apostles. All who believed were together and had all things in common...*" (Acts 2:43–44).

So, how did the apostle Paul disciple the many new believers around him? He travelled with groups of disciples. When Paul went on his missionary adventures, people came with him. We read in sacred Scripture that Barnabas, Luke, Titus, and Timothy were all among those who travelled with Paul. While Paul may have spent individual time with men such as Titus or Timothy, he clearly invested his time to create a community of disciples. It takes a village to make a disciple.

How do we participate in a community of believers? We read in the First Book of Peter:

> *Above all, maintain constant love for one another, for love covers a multitude of sins. Be hospitable to one another without complaining. Like good stewards of the manifold grace of God, serve one another with whatever gift each of you has received. Whoever speaks must do so as one speaking the very words of God; whoever serves must do so with the strength that God supplies, so that God may be glorified in all things through Jesus Christ. To him belong the glory and the power forever and ever. Amen* (1 Peter 4:8–11).

My friends, the overarching benefit of being involved in community and practicing our faith in community, can be found in the Gospel according to St. Matthew, where he instructs us that, *"If two of you agree on earth about anything you ask, it will be done for you by my Father in heaven. For where two or three are gathered in my name, I am there among them"* (Matthew 18:19–20).

Let us pray:

> Holy Lord,
> who sent Your only Son Jesus Christ to be crucified for
> our sins,
> have mercy on me.
>
> Give me the grace to follow in His example,
> leading and loving in great humility,
> for You oppose the proud but raise up the humble.
>
> Help me to be humble and gracious in every interaction;
> patient, loving, and kind.
>
> I humble myself before You, Lord,
> for I am nothing without You.
>
> I long to serve You, Lord, and follow in Your way.
>
> Amen.

Chapter Six

Practice of the Faith arising from the Mediterranean-Abrahamic Religions

Abrahamic religions symbol designating the three prevalent monotheistic religions – Judaism, Christianity, and Islam

Three of the major world religions are very closely related both in their origins and in their sacred Scripture. They also have very similar beliefs about morals and ethics. They do differ, however, in important aspects of their beliefs. Historically, relations among these faith groups reflect both times of conflict and times of cooperation. In modern times, adherents of the Abrahamic religions sometimes seem to be enemies and aliens. At other times, they seem like squabbling children of a single parent who are, in fact, capable of reaching shared understandings and living in peace, moving toward building a world of religious cooperation.

The Abrahamic religions refer to three monotheistic religions: Judaism, Christianity, and Islam, which account for more than half of the world's total population today. Although tending to decline in terms of global population, those who identify with Christianity account for 32.5% of the world's population. While tending to increase in terms of global percentage, those who identify with Islam account for 21.5% of the world's population. Those who identify with Judaism account for 0.2% of the world's population.

Judaism, Christianity, and Islam are called Abrahamic religions because they each accept the tradition of the God (known as Yahweh in Hebrew and Allah in Arabic) that revealed Himself to Abraham. The theological traditions of the Abrahamic religions are influenced by the depiction of the God of Israel in the Hebrew Bible, by the story of Abraham, and acclaimed as the father of monotheism in the history of Judaism.

The Abrahamic God is shared as a linchpin among all three traditions. The expression "Abrahamic religions" is used to express the fact that these three monotheistic religions claim Abraham as their forefather in common and, thereby, share a common heritage. The prophet Abraham is claimed by Jews as the ancestor of the Israelites, while his son Ishmael is viewed in Muslim tradition as the ancestor of the Arabs. In Christian tradition, Abraham is described as a "father in faith."

According to sacred Scripture, the patriarch Abraham (or *Ibrahim,* in Arabic) had eight sons by three wives: one (Ishmael) by his wife's servant Hagar, one (Isaac) by his wife Sarah, and six by another wife, Keturah. Ishmael, a son of Abraham, becomes the father of the Muslim people. According to Muslim tradition, Ishmael the

Patriarch and his mother Hagar are buried next to the Kaaba in the Holy City of Mecca.[117]

Isaac, another son of Abraham, becomes one of the patriarchs of the Jewish people. In short, the Jewish faithful see Abraham as the progenitor of the people of Israel through his descendants Isaac and Jacob. Christians view Abraham as an important exemplar of faith and a spiritual, as well as a physical, ancestor of Jesus.

Muslims refer to Christians and Jews as "People of the Book" ("the Book" referring to the Tanakh[118], the New Testament, and the Qur'an (Koran)).[119] Muslims see Abraham as one of the most important of the many prophets sent by God. Thus, Abraham represents, for some, a point of commonality that they seek to emphasize by means of this terminology.

For the Jewish faithful, Father Abraham is a revered ancestor, or patriarch, to whom God made several promises, including that he would have numberless descendants and that they would receive the land of Canaan (the Promised Land). Abraham is known as the first post-flood person to reject idolatry. Hence, he symbolically appears as a fundamental figure for monotheistic religion.

For Christians, Abraham is a spiritual forebear rather than a direct ancestor. For example, Christian iconography depicts him as an early witness to the Trinity in the form of three angels who visited

---

117 Gibb, Hamilton A.R., & Kramers, J. H. (1965). *Shorter encyclopaedia of Islam*. Cornell University Press.

118 The Tanakh is a name used in Judaism for the canon of the Hebrew Bible, comprising the books of law, the prophets, and collected writings. The Books of the Christian Old Testament closely approximate, but have important distinctions from, the Jewish Tanakh.

119 The Qur'an, literally meaning "the recitation," is the sacred text of Islam, considered by Muslims to contain the revelations of God (Allah) to Muhammad.

him (Genesis 18:2).[120] In Christian belief, Abraham is a model of faith. His intention to obey God by offering up Isaac is seen as a foreshadowing of God's offering of His son, Jesus.

In Islam, Ibrahim (Abraham) is considered part of a line of prophets beginning with Adam. He is the "first Muslim," that is, the first monotheist in a world where monotheism was lost. Islam holds that it was Ishmael rather than Isaac whom Ibrahim was instructed to sacrifice.

So, let's begin there, with the Biblical account of the offering of Isaac. It is found in the first Book of sacred Scripture, the Book of Genesis. It's the story of a man and his son walking up Mount Moriah. The young man is bent under the weight of the wood for a burnt offering, and the father is striding behind, carrying the fire and the knife.

After these things God tested Abraham. He said to him, "Abraham!" And he said, "Here I am." He said, "Take your son, your only son Isaac, whom you love, and go to the land of Moriah, and offer him there as a burnt offering on one of the mountains that I shall show you."

So Abraham rose early in the morning, saddled his donkey, and took two of his young men with him, and his son Isaac; he cut the wood for the burnt offering, and set out and went to the place in the distance that God had shown him. On the third day Abraham looked up and saw the place far away.

Then Abraham said to his young men, "Stay here with the donkey; the boy and I will go over there; we will

120 Holy Bible: New Revised Standard Version. (1993). Catholic Bible Press.

worship, and then we will come back to you." Abraham took the wood of the burnt offering and laid it on his son Isaac, and he himself carried the fire and the knife. So the two of them walked on together. Isaac said to his father Abraham, "Father!" And he said, "Here I am, my son." He said, "The fire and the wood are here, but where is the lamb for a burnt offering?" Abraham said, "God himself will provide the lamb for a burnt offering, my son." So the two of them walked on together.

When they came to the place that God had shown him, Abraham built an altar there and laid the wood in order. He bound his son Isaac, and laid him on the altar, on top of the wood. Then Abraham reached out his hand and took the knife to kill his son.

But the angel of the Lord called to him from heaven, and said, "Abraham, Abraham!" And he said, "Here I am." He said, "Do not lay your hand on the boy or do anything to him; for now I know that you fear God, since you have not withheld your son, your only son, from me."

And Abraham looked up and saw a ram, caught in a thicket by its horns. Abraham went and took the ram and offered it up as a burnt offering instead of his son. So Abraham called that place "The Lord will provide"; as it is said to this day, "On the mount of the Lord it shall be provided." The angel of the Lord called to Abraham a second time from heaven, and said, "By myself I have sworn," says the Lord: "Because you have done this, and have not withheld your son, your only son, I will indeed bless you, and I will make your offspring as numerous as the stars of heaven and as the sand that is on the seashore. And your offspring shall possess the gate of their enemies, and by your offspring shall all the nations of the earth gain blessing for themselves, because you have obeyed my voice" (Genesis 22:1–18).

Abraham is about to slay his son, not as an act of cruelty or rage, but out of total and complete obedience to his God. This raises so many questions.

- What kind of God would ask a man to do this?

- What kind of man would obey?

- What if Isaac had been our son, the fulfillment of an impossible promise?

- Could we have travelled for three days through barren territory, arriving at the foot of Mount Moriah dreading the moment and yet walking steadily toward it?

The questions betray our limited understanding. Seeing the story through human eyes, we miss the point. We fail to see what it means to be God and what it means to be human.

Why would God ask for such a sacrifice? Because there is no other way for us to learn that He is God. When we put something on God's altar, when we lay it at the foot of the cross, we acknowledge two things. One, we acknowledge that Yahweh is God ... that Elohim[121] is God. And two, we acknowledge that we are not God.

Each of us will be faced with Abraham's dilemma, perhaps many times in our lives. In our case—God willing—it won't be a matter of physically placing a child on the altar, but it may mean placing a child in God's hands and God's hands alone. If not a child, then something else—a relationship, a career, or a dream. Whatever it is, if we offer it to God as Abraham offered his only son, we will begin to know God as the loving Father who provides for our every need.

God tells Abraham to offer Isaac: "*Take now your son, your only son Isaac, whom you love, and go to the land of Moriah and offer him there as a burnt offering on one of the mountains of which I shall tell you*" (Genesis 22:2). This is a foundational event both for Judaism and for Christianity. Judaism sees these events as a testing of Abraham's faith. Christianity, on the other hand, understands it as a signpost, pointing to the most significant event in all history, when another Father would offer His only Son upon that same mountain.[122]

In the story of Abraham and Isaac as father and son, Holy Mother Church sees images of God the Father and God the Son. The offering of Isaac points us forward in time to the redeeming sacrifice of Jesus upon the cross. That this is true can be seen from any number

---

121 Elohim is the Hebrew word for God that appears in the very first sentence of sacred Scripture. This ancient name for God, as the One who began it all, contains the idea of God's creative power as well as His authority and sovereignty.

122 According to Jewish tradition, King Solomon built the first Jewish Temple on Mount Moriah, commemorating the exact spot where Abraham stretched out Isaac upon the altar of sacrifice. Golgotha, the place of Christ's crucifixion, is located just outside the walls of Jerusalem, not more than 700 m from the spot where King Solomon built the first Jewish Temple. Mount Moriah, the Temple of Solomon, the place of Isaac's intended sacrifice, and Golgotha are all the same place. All mark the place where God bound Himself to fulfill the promises of the Abrahamic Covenant.

of correlations between the testing of Abraham and the crucifixion of Jesus. Let's look at some of those correlations.

- Abraham offered his only son, Isaac. God offered his only Son, Jesus.

- Mount Moriah was to become the future site of the Holy City of Jerusalem. As Abraham was to sacrifice Isaac on a mountain in Moriah, God would later allow Jesus to be sacrificed on that same mountain just outside the Temple Mount at Jerusalem.

- After travelling three days through barren territory to arrive at the foot of Mount Moriah, Isaac escaped death. After journeying into the bowels of hell, Jesus rose from the dead on the third day.

- As Abraham placed the wood for the sacrifice on Isaac's shoulders, so God allowed the wooden cross to be placed upon the shoulders of His only Son. In the same way that Isaac cried out to his father, Jesus too cried out to His Father.

- In place of Isaac, God provided a ram that day. But there would come, centuries later, another lamb, a Lamb that would die for the entire human race. Jesus Christ, the Lamb of God. And again, God provided the Lamb.

- The ram was caught by its horns, by its head, in a thicket of thorns. Jesus was forced to wear a crown made of thorns.

- Isaac had committed no wrong. He was innocent of anything that called for his death. Jesus too was absolutely innocent.

- Isaac willingly obeyed his father by accepting the ropes with which he was tied. Of His own free will, Jesus offered Himself as a sacrifice, in obedience to the will of the Father.

Despite the similarities between these two accounts, there is one critical difference. The difference is seen in the endings. Isaac was saved from death. Jesus went through death and emerged victorious on the other side. Both acted according to God's plan for our salvation.

Let us pray:

> Father God,
> Thank You for the example of Abraham, for his obedience and his trust in you.
> Grow our faith so that we also trust in you and offer you the best of ourselves.
>
> Amen.

Judaism, Christianity, and Islam each agree on several significant principles. They include:

- **Monotheism**. All three religions worship one God. While Jews and Muslims sometimes criticize the common Christian doctrine of the Holy Trinity as polytheistic, there exists a general understanding that all three religions worship the same one God.

- **A prophetic tradition.** All three religions recognize figures called "prophets," though their lists differ, as do their interpretations of the prophetic role.

- **Semitic origins.** Judaism and Islam originated among Semitic peoples—namely the Jews and Arabs, respectively—while Christianity arose out of Judaism.

- **A basis in divine revelation.** Rather than, for example, philosophical speculation or custom.

- **An ethical orientation.** All three religions speak of a choice between good and evil, which is juxtaposed with obedience or disobedience to God.

- **A linear concept of history.** Beginning with God's creation and the concept that God works through history.

- **Association with the desert.** Some commentators believe this association has imbued these religions with a particular ethos.

- **Devotion to the traditions.** As found in the Tanakh, the Bible, and the Qur'an, such as the stories of Adam, Noah, Abraham, and Moses.

In the Christian and Jewish traditions, God is conceived of as having several attributes, which include:

- **God is omnipotent**

  Omnipotent means to have unlimited power. God can do anything He wills without any effort on His part. It's important to note the "anything He wills" part of that statement, because

God cannot do anything that is contradictory or contrary to His nature.

In his devotional *Forward*,[123] Ron Moore puts it this way. He says that when God plans something for your life, He is not dependent on circumstances, your strength, your network, or the economy. He is not wringing His hands, hoping that you are in the right place at the right time. God's will is not reliant on the circumstances of mere mortals. God has great plans for you, and He'll get them done.

- **God is omniscient**

  Omniscient means to have infinite awareness, understanding, and insight. God, being the source and author of all things, knows all that can be known. And this He knows with a fullness of perfection that includes every possible item of knowledge concerning everything that exists or could have existed anywhere in the universe at any time in the past or that may exist in the centuries or ages yet to come.

  We read in the Book of Isaiah that God says, "*Remember the former things of old; for I am God, and there is no other; I am God, and there is no one like me, declaring the end from the beginning and from ancient times things not yet done, saying, 'My purpose shall stand, and I will fulfill my intention'*" (Isaiah 46:9–10).

- **God is omnipresent**

  Omnipresence means that God is always everywhere. The fullness of His presence is all around us. The psalmist recounts:

---

123 https://www.crosswalk.com/devotionals/forward/forward-with-ron-moore-july-17-2017.html

"Where can I go from your spirit? Or where can I flee from your presence? If I ascend to heaven, you are there; if I make my bed in Sheol, you are there. If I take the wings of the morning and settle at the farthest limits of the sea, even there your hand shall lead me, and your right hand shall hold me fast" (Psalm 139:7–10).

Spiritual writer Debbie McDaniel writes this about the omnipresence of God: *"He can be everywhere, at the same time. And He never sleeps or slumbers. He's aware every moment of every day, exactly what we're up against. He knows our way, and is with us always. There's no place on this earth we can go that He doesn't see and know of."*[124]

- **God is infinite**

Infinite means that God self-exists without origin. The fact that God is self-existent— that He was created by nothing and has always existed forever—is perhaps one of the hardest attributes of God for the believer to understand. In our limitedness, grasping the nature of a limitless God is like holding onto water as it rages down a river.

Evangelical author A. W. Tozer[125] writes this about the confusing, head-spinning attribute of God's infinity: *"To admit that there is One who lies beyond us, who exists outside of all our categories, who will not be dismissed with a name, who will not appear before the bar of our reason, nor submit to our curious inquiries: this requires a great deal of humility, more than most of us possess, so we save face by thinking God down to our level, or at least down to where we can manage Him."*

---

124 https://www.crosswalk.com/blogs/debbie-mcdaniel/what-the-enemy-doesnt-want-you-to-know-3-things-he-cant-do-that-only-god-can.html

125 Tozer, A. W. (2009). *The knowledge of the holy.* Library of Congress.

- **God is omni-benevolent**

Omni-benevolence means to possess perfect or unlimited goodness. God is infinitely and unchangingly kind and full of good will toward us, His creatures.

When the psalmist writes, *"O taste and see that the Lord is good; happy are those who take refuge in him"* (Psalm 34:8), he is inviting us not just to believe that God is good, but also to experience God's goodness. According to Tozer,[126] the goodness of God *"disposes Him to be kind, cordial, benevolent, and full of good will toward men. He is tender-hearted and of quick sympathy, and His unfailing attitude toward all moral beings is open, frank, and friendly. By His nature He is inclined to bestow blessedness and He takes holy pleasure in the happiness of His people."*

- **God is merciful.**

Without the mercy of God, we would have no hope of heaven. Because of our disobedient hearts, we deserve death. We read in St. Paul's Letter to the Church in Rome that *"..there is no distinction, since all have sinned and fall short of the glory of God; they are now justified by his grace as a gift, through the redemption that is in Christ Jesus..."* (Romans 3:22–24), and *"For the wages of sin is death, but the free gift of God is eternal life in Christ Jesus our Lord"* (Romans 6:23). Because of mercy, we don't get what we deserve. Instead, because of the mercy of God, we get life through faith in Christ.

Tozer[127] writes this about the mercy of God. *"As judgment is God's justice confronting moral inequity, so mercy is the*

---

126 Tozer, A. W. (2009). *The knowledge of the holy.* Library of Congress.
127 Tozer, A. W. (2009). *The knowledge of the holy.* Library of Congress.

goodness of God confronting human suffering and guilt. Were there no guilt in the world, no pain and no tears, God would yet be infinitely merciful; but His mercy might well remain hidden in His heart, unknown to the created universe. No voice would be raised to celebrate the mercy of which none felt the need. It is human misery and sin that call forth the divine mercy."

- **God is gracious**

He is infinitely inclined to spare the guilty. The psalmist tells us that, *"The Lord is gracious and merciful, slow to anger and abounding in steadfast love"* (Psalm 145:8).

If mercy is not getting what we do deserve (damnation), grace is getting what we don't deserve (eternal life). *"As mercy is God's goodness confronting human misery and guilt,"* Tozer writes, *"so grace is His goodness directed toward human debt and demerit. It is by His grace that God imputes merit where none previously existed and declares no debt to be where one had been before."*[128]

- **God is holy**

"And the four living creatures, each of them with six wings, are full of eyes all around and inside. Day and night without ceasing they sing, 'Holy, holy, holy, the Lord God the Almighty, who was and is and is to come'" (Revelation 4:8).

The word *"holy"* means sacred, set apart, revered, or divine. And yet none of those words is adequate to describe the awesome holiness of our God. John MacArthur writes this about God's holiness: *"Of all the attributes of God, holiness is the one that most uniquely describes Him and in reality, is a summation of*

---

128 Tozer, A. W. (2009). *The knowledge of the holy.* Library of Congress.

all His other attributes. The word holiness refers to His separateness, His otherness, the fact that He is unlike any other being. It indicates His complete and infinite perfection. Holiness is the attribute of God that binds all the others together."[129]

That God is holy means He is endlessly, always perfect. And His standard for us is perfection as well. Jesus calls us to *"Be perfect, therefore, as your heavenly Father is perfect"* (Matthew 5:48). That's why we need Christ. Without Christ taking the place for us and dying for our sins, we would all fall short of God's holy standard.

- **God is wisdom**

God is infinitely wise, consistently wise, perfectly wise. Tozer writes, *"Wisdom, among other things, is the ability to devise perfect ends and to achieve those ends by the most perfect means. It sees the end from the beginning, so there can be no need to guess or conjecture. Wisdom sees everything in focus, each in proper relation to all, and is thus able to work toward predestined goals with flawless precision."*[130]

Indeed, when we see wisdom like this, we realize just how much our limited, finite wisdom compares with the limitless, infinite wisdom of God. And how comforting and wonderful this is for us to dwell on! The fact that God can never be wiser means He is always doing the wisest thing in our lives. No plan we could make for our lives could be better than the plan He has already crafted and is carrying out for us. We might not understand His ways today. But we can trust that, because God is infinitely wise, He truly is working all things

---

129 https://www.gty.org/library/sermons-library/GTY100/The-Holiness-of-God
130 Tozer, A. W. (2009). *The knowledge of the holy.* Library of Congress.

out in the best possible way for our good and the good of the whole world.

- **God is just**

He is infinitely and unchangeably right and perfect in all that He does. We read in the Book of Deuteronomy, *"The Rock, his work is perfect, and all his ways are just. A faithful God, without deceit, just and upright is he"* (Deuteronomy 32:4).

What does it mean that God is just? Surely, it means more than He is simply fair. It means that He always does what is right and good toward all people. To that end, a natural question that arises is how then can a just God justify the unjust? Tozer answers this by reminding us that we find the answer through the Christian doctrine of justification and redemption. Tozer says, *"Through the work of Christ in atonement, justice is not violated but satisfied when God spares a sinner."*[131] His mercy does not forbid Him to exercise his justice, nor does His justice forbid Him to exercise His mercy. He is both fully merciful and fully just.

In light of God's other attributes of goodness, mercy, love, and grace, there are some who might, in error, say that God is too kind to punish the ungodly. But to believe this means we dull the reality of His infinite, unchanging justice. God will have justice for sin, either from Christ's atoning death, or, for those who will not accept it, eternal wrath in damnation. Sproul explains it this way: *"Let's assume that all men are guilty of sin in the sight of God. From the mass of humanity, God sovereignly decides to give mercy to some of them. What do the rest get?*

---

131 Tozer, A. W. (2009). *The knowledge of the holy.* Library of Congress.

They get justice. The saved get mercy and the unsaved get justice. Nobody gets injustice."[132]

- **God is immutable**

    To be immutable means to be not subject or susceptible to change; unalterable. God's attributes are the same from before the beginning of time into eternity. His character never changes. His plans do not change. His promises do not change. What all this means, very simply, is that God is dependable! Our trust in Him is therefore a confident trust, for we know that He will not, indeed, He cannot, change.

    His purposes are unfailing, His promises unassailable. It is because the God who promised us eternal life is immutable that we may rest assured that nothing, *"not trouble or hardship or persecution or famine or nakedness or danger or sword shall separate us from the love of Christ"* (Romans 8:35). It is because Jesus Christ is the same yesterday, today, and forever that *"neither angels nor demons, neither the present nor the future, not even powers, height, depth, nor anything else in all creation, will be able to separate us from the love of God that is in Christ Jesus our Lord"* (Romans 8:38–39).

- And, above all else, **God is love**

    God infinitely and unchangingly loves us, His creatures. We read in the Holy Gospel, *"Beloved, let us love one another, because love is from God; everyone who loves is born of God*

---

132 https://www.ligonier.org/learn/series/holiness_of_god/holiness-and-justice/

and knows God. Whoever does not love does not know God, for God is love" (1 John 4:7–8).

As with all attributes, we can only begin to comprehend God's love in light of His other attributes. The love of God is eternal, sovereign, unchanging, and infinite. *"It is a strange and beautiful eccentricity of the free God,"* Tozer writes, *"that He has allowed His heart to be emotionally identified with men. Self-sufficient as He is, He wants our love and will not be satisfied till He gets it. Free as He is, He has let His heart be bound to us forever. God's love is active, drawing us to Himself. His love is personal. He doesn't love humanity in some vague sense, He loves humans. He loves you and me. And His love for us knows no beginning and no end."*[133]

This, this is the God we adore,
Our faithful, unchangeable Friend,
Whose love is as great as His power,
And knows neither measure nor end.

'Tis Jesus, the first and the last,
Whose Spirit shall guide us safe home;
We praise Him for all that is past,
And trust Him for all that's to come.

Joseph Hart[134]

---

133 Tozer, A. W. (2009). *The knowledge of the holy.* Library of Congress.
134 Hart, Joseph. (2015) Lyrics from *Thou Shepherd of Israel—A Ranter Tune. S. A. Songbook*, Edition #1041. <u>usawest.org</u>.

All three Abrahamic religions rely on a body of scriptures. Some of those works are the Word of God, hence sacred and unquestionable. Some of those works are the work of religious people, revered mainly by tradition and to the extent that they are considered to have been divinely inspired, if not dictated, by the Divine Being.

The sacred Scripture of Christians is the Holy Bible, which is divided into two main sections, the Old Testament and the New Testament. The Old Testament begins with the creation of the world and then follows the story through the great flood; the call of Abraham; the forming of the holy nation of Israel and the settling thereof, exile from, and return to the Promised Land. It contains writings from the great kings David and Solomon, as well as from many of Israel's great prophets, both minor prophets and major prophets.

The New Testament opens with the four Gospels: Matthew, Mark, Luke, and John, which are biographies. They are recollections of the birth, life, death, and resurrection of Jesus Christ. The New Testament also contains letters written by the apostles to particular individuals and churches. The letters of St. Paul are a primary example.

There are different translations of the Bible. This does not mean that the books and the passages say different things. Far from it; there is only one Bible. The one distinction which exists among the different translations of the Holy Bible is a canonical distinction.

In some translations, there are a different number of books contained in the Old Testament, in the Hebrew Scriptures. In the Roman Catholic and Orthodox Churches, the Old Testament Canon is based on the Septuagint, which is a Greek translation of Jewish Scripture. The result is that these versions of the Bible have more

Old Testament books (46) than most Protestant versions (39) of the Bible. The Protestant, Catholic, and Orthodox New Testaments are identical.

The Jewish Bible—the *Tanakh*—is the same as the Christian Old Testament, except for its book arrangement. The first five books are called the Law, or the Pentateuch (Genesis, Exodus, Leviticus, Numbers, and Deuteronomy), which were written or edited primarily by Moses in the early 1400s BC (Deuteronomy 31:9–13). These books are known as the Torah. The books of the Hebrew Bible are arranged by topic, including the Law (or the Torah), the Prophets (or Nebiim), and the Writings (or Kethubim).

For Christians, the books of the Old Testament are arranged in a different sequence. First the Books of the Law: Genesis, Exodus, Leviticus, Numbers, and Deuteronomy. Then the Wisdom writings: Judges, Samuel, Kings, First and Second Chronicles, the Psalms, and Proverbs. As Christians, our Canon places the writings of the prophets at the end of the Old Testament. This arrangement of the texts is because, for Christians, the prophets point the way to the New Testament. They proclaim the coming of the New Covenant, Jesus Christ.

The Bible is not a single book, but rather a collection of smaller books and letters, much like our modern-day libraries. Like any library, the Bible contains many kinds of literature written by different people at different times and for different purposes. There are stories, songs, poetry, history, prophetic visions, and religious teachings.

The Bible is an ancient collection of writings comprised of 73 separate books written over approximately 1,600 years by at least 40 distinct authors. The Old Testament contains 46 books (or 39 books depending on the translation) written from approximately 1500 to 400 years before the birth of Christ. The New Testament contains 27 books written from approximately 40 to 90 years after Christ's birth.

This corpus is divinely inspired. The roots of our Christian faith draw from the Jewish faith. Like our Jewish forefathers, as Christians we believe that the Bible is the inspired Word of God. As Christians, when we speak of the Bible as inspired, we are referring to the fact that God divinely influenced the human authors of the scriptures in such a way that what they wrote was the very Word of God.

In the Book of Second Timothy, we read, "*All scripture is inspired by God and is useful for teaching, for reproof, for correction, and for training in righteousness, so that everyone who belongs to God may be proficient, equipped for every good work*" (2 Timothy 3:16–17). This verse tells us that God inspired all scripture and that it is profitable to us. It is not just the parts of the Bible that deal with religious doctrines that are inspired, but each and every word from Genesis to Revelation. Because it is inspired by God, the scriptures are authoritative in establishing doctrine and teaching its readers how to be in right relationship with God.

Another passage which speaks to the inspiration of the scriptures is: "*First of all you must understand this, that no prophecy of scripture is a matter of one's own interpretation, because no prophecy ever came by human will, but men and women moved by the Holy Spirit spoke from God*" (2 Peter 1:20–21). This verse helps us to understand that even though God used people with their distinctive personalities and writing styles, God divinely inspired the very words they wrote.

Holy Mother Church teaches that God inspired the content to the writer, but He did not prevent the writer's natural abilities. God did not somehow bind the writer's mind or will. Each author's personality is perceptible in the Books of sacred Scripture. The experienced reader would never mistake Isaiah for Jeremiah, or Mark for John, because each inspired writer still had their own style and approach to language.

Jesus Himself confirmed this inspiration of the scriptures when He said, "*Do not think that I have come to abolish the law or the prophets; I have come not to abolish but to fulfill. For truly I tell you, until heaven and earth pass away, not one letter, not one stroke of a letter, will pass from the law until all is accomplished ...*" (Matthew 5:17–18). In these verses, Jesus is reinforcing the accuracy of the scriptures down to the smallest detail, because it is the very Word of God.

As mentioned earlier, the Jewish Bible—the *Tanakh*—is the sacred scriptures of Judaism. These are complemented by, and supplemented with, various originally oral traditions: *Midrash,* the *Mishnah,* the *Talmud,* and collected rabbinical writings. The Hebrew text of the Tanakh, and the Torah in particular, is considered holy.

Islam's holiest book is the Qur'an, comprised of 114 surahs, or chapters. Muslims also believe in the religious texts of Judaism and Christianity in their original forms and not the current versions, which they believe to be corrupted. According to the Qur'an (and mainstream Muslim belief), the verses of the Qur'an were revealed from Allah through the Archangel Gabriel to the Prophet Muhammad on separate occasions. These revelations were written down during Muhammad's lifetime and collected into one official copy in 633 CE.

The Qur'an mentions several of the Israelite prophets, including Jesus. The stories of these prophets are very similar to those in the Bible. However, in Islam, the detailed precepts of the Tanakh and the New Testament are not adopted outright. Instead, they are replaced by the new commandments revealed directly by God (through Gabriel) to Muhammad and codified in the Qur'an.

Muslims consider the original Arabic text of the Qur'an as uncorrupted and holy to the last letter. Translations are interpretations of the meaning of the Qur'an, as only the original Arabic text is considered to be the divine scripture. The Qur'an is complemented by the *Hadith,* a set of books by later authors that record the sayings of the Prophet Muhammad.

The Abrahamic religions also share an expectation of an individual who will herald the end times and/or bring about the Kingdom of God on Earth, in other words, the fulfillment of Messianic prophecy. Judaism awaits the coming of the Jewish Messiah. Christianity awaits the second coming of Christ. Islam awaits both the second coming of Jesus (in order to complete His life and die, since he is said to have been risen alive and not crucified) and the coming of Mahdi, the expected messiah of Muslim tradition.

The Abrahamic religions concur that a human being comprises the body, which dies, and the soul, which need not do so. The soul, capable of remaining alive beyond human death, carries the essence of that person with it, and God will judge that person's life accordingly after the physical body dies. The importance of this, the focus on it, and the precise criteria and end result, differs among religions.

So, what does all of this mean for the religious and spiritual life of the older adult who identifies with one of the three Abrahamic religions? Well, my friends, this is good news! The secular view of human beings is that of self-contained vessels that lose their value when drained of society's all-important characteristics of self-awareness, the ability to communicate in ways others understand, independent functioning, and so forth. However, the Abrahamic religions (Judaism, Christianity, and Islam) call us back to:

- a lively awareness of the centrality of relationship for genuine well-being;

- the need for human solidarity in the face of the myriad and inevitable disabilities that everyone will eventually face; and

- the inherent worth of persons whom the larger society has labeled "disabled" or "old" and, therefore, of no further value to the greater society.

All three of the Abrahamic religions assert that the human condition must be acknowledged if one is to be in right relationship with God. That is, if one is to recognize his or her utter and total dependence upon God and God's gracious provision for humankind. As understood by the Abrahamic religions, the root of all our problems lies precisely in the belief that we have no need of community but, rather, can go it alone and be totally autonomous and self-sufficient.

In fact, those with disabilities or dementia may function as a reminder of God's grace to us. The unavoidable dependence that often accompanies growing old, and certainly is a given for those with disability or dementia, is satisfied through the grace of serving one another as Christ served us.

The literature affirms that those who practice a religion have less death anxiety and fare better as they grow old and face mortality. The proposed answer lies in the unique and specific rituals of repentance embedded in the Abrahamic religions, transcending the idea that social support and the belief in an afterlife are the only factors involved. The religious concept of repentance requires reviewing and examining one's personal life. This is a well-accepted mental health process reported in psychological studies and confirmed by palliative care professionals to be associated with transforming personal attitudes and behaviour and helping to find the meaning and purpose of life, thus easing death anxiety.

The Jewish tradition of leaving an ethical legacy, the performance of Christian liturgy, and the practice of Islamic ritual prayer all give space for—and equip a person with—a formal way to look back, examine, and testify to others about transformative life experiences, not just at the end of life, but over a lifetime. The significance of rituals of repentance not only lies in how they facilitate the possibility of living a good and peaceful death, they are also the only way to transform the greater society.

In Psalm 23, King David tells us:

> *The Lord is my shepherd, I shall not want. He makes me lie down in green pastures; he leads me beside still waters; he restores my soul. He leads me in right paths for his name's sake. Even though I walk through the darkest valley, I fear no evil; for you are with me; your rod and your staff—they comfort me. You prepare a table before me in the presence of my enemies; you anoint my head with oil; my cup overflows. Surely*

goodness and mercy shall follow me all the days of my life, and I shall dwell in the house of the Lord my whole life long (Psalm 23:1–6).

King David says, "*Even though I walk through the valley of the shadow of death, I will fear no evil ....*" This is death, remember. Death—the great enemy of humankind, the place that every person will go, and go alone. Death stands off in the darkness, hunkering down in the shadows of our lives like a monster. It is terrible, lonely, and fearful. But *God is with us even there.* As King David says, even there—as I face death—I will not fear, because God is with me.

So, what does that mean for us here and now? My friends, it means that if God is with us in the moment of our greatest trial, in the shadow of death, He will be with us in all the other afflictions of our lives. Painful as they are, as dark as the night may get, we know it is not too painful for God. No obstacle is too dark for Him to overcome.

God is there as we walk through the valley of the shadow of death, and He is there in every valley along the way. His grace will find us. That grace which saw us before the foundation of the world was laid; that grace which spoke creation into existence; that grace which walked with Jesus to the cross—that grace will abound for us in eternity. God's grace will find us.

It doesn't matter who you are or where you are. No matter where you've gone or how far you've drifted from God's loving embrace, nowhere is out of His reach. God in His grace is able to be there with you. Amid pain and uncertainty, in the high of blessing and cheer, God is with you. His grace will find you, wherever you may be.

St. Patrick's Breastplate is a popular prayer attributed to one of Ireland's most beloved patron saints. According to tradition, St. Patrick wrote it in 433 A.D. for divine protection before successfully converting the Irish King Leoghaire and his subjects from paganism to Christianity. Let us pray:

> I bind unto myself today,
> the power of God to hold and lead,
> His eye to watch, His might to stay,
> His ear to hearken to my need:
> the wisdom of my God to teach,
> His hand to guide, His shield to ward;
> the Word of God to give me speech,
> His heavenly host to be my guard.
>
> Christ be with me, Christ within me,
> Christ behind me, Christ before me,
> Christ beside me, Christ to win me,
> Christ to comfort and restore me,
> Christ beneath me, Christ above me,
> Christ in quiet, Christ in danger,
> Christ in hearts of all that love me,
> Christ in mouth of friend and stranger.
>
> I bind myself to God's power to guide me, God's might to uphold me,
> God's wisdom to teach me, God's Eye to watch over me,
> God's Ear to hear me, God's way to lie before me,

God's shield to shelter me, God's host to secure me ... against the snares of demons, against the seductions of vices, against the lusts of nature, against everyone who meditates injury to me, whether far or near, few or many.[135]

---

135 St. Patrick's Breastplate. Patron Saint of Ireland. (ca. 389–461 AD.)

Chapter Seven

How Religious and Spiritual Practices Affect Our Health

Look around most congregations at worship and witness the courage and persistence of the aged men and women who arrive with walkers and oxygen tanks, often transported by other older people less encumbered by health problems. Sharing pews with noisy babies, children with crayons, bored teens, and distracted parents, they sing and pray, sit in silence, listen to scripture and sermons, rise and sit as they are able, share the Eucharist if Christian, and exit in friendly conversation with fellow travelers. In the hymns, prayers, scripture readings, and sermons, they hear of love and forgiveness, gratitude and hope, despair and lamentation, anger, fear, and awe. In no other community do persons of so many different backgrounds and ages meet regularly to consider the human condition and turn to the sacred for an enduring sense of meaning and purpose in life.[136]

---

136 Kimble, M. and McFadden, S. (2002). *Aging, Spirituality, and Religion: A Handbook, Volume 2.* Fortress Press.

In an earlier chapter, I identified that for older adults in particular a growing body of research is demonstrating that religious and spiritual practices may be positively associated with improved physical and mental health, increased longevity, and stronger social support systems.

By definition, *religion* is a personal set or institutionalized system of religious attitudes, beliefs, and practices—the service and worship of God or the supernatural.[137] Spirituality, on the other hand, has no single, widely agreed-upon definition. In our world today, the emphasis of spirituality is on subjective experience and the deepest values and meanings by which people live, incorporating personal growth and transformation, usually in a context separate from organized religious institutions.[138]

One of the hallmarks of religion is its organization, a structured, frequently rule-based construct that to some degree governs the behaviour of its members. Moral rules, laws, and doctrines, as well as specific codes and criteria, create the organized structure that contains the religion's specific belief system. This isn't necessarily a bad thing. In uncertain times, the rules and dogma of organized religion help to give society a sense of certainty and comfort.

Spirituality, on the other hand, breaks free from the restrictions and rigid structure sometimes associated with traditional religion. Rather than following a set of external rules, the spiritual aspirant is following their own inner call. In this way, spirituality can sometimes feel like a rebellious act of going solo and leaving the tribe, very much in the spirit of American philosopher and poet Ralph

---

137 https://www.merriam-webster.com/dictionary/religion
138 Sheldrake, Philip. (2007). *A brief history of spirituality*. Wiley-Blackwell.

Waldo Emerson when he spoke of being yourself in a world that is constantly trying to make you something else.

While religious beliefs and spiritual experiences differ in the ways in which they are practiced, each serves as a vehicle to lead one closer to the truth of which they seek. And, each of these routes—religion and spirituality—can have positive benefits on our health and well-being. A growing body of research is beginning to define the complex connections between religious and spiritual beliefs and practices and an individual's physical and psychological health. No one says it's as simple as going to services or "finding religion" later in life. It may be that people who are more involved in religious activities or who are more spiritual are doing something that makes them feel better emotionally and helps them live longer and more healthily. The question, researchers say, is what exactly are they doing?

Through a discussion of current research and related observations, Idler[139] highlights many of the positive benefits that religious and spiritual practices can have on one's health and well-being. Starting at an early age, Idler says, the choices one makes based on spiritual beliefs and values directly relate to the creation of certain lifestyle habits, such as diet, alcohol use, and sexual practices. Moreover, the benefit of a religious community made up of a variety of individuals from many generations also provides a strong sense of support and connection. The overall effect of such practices on one's health and well-being is found to be positive over a lifetime.

Meditation, yoga, fasting, walking a prayer circle, making a pilgrimage, taking the sacraments, singing with a choir, going on a weekend

---

139 Idler, Ellen. (2008). Spirituality. *Higher education newsletter*, February 2008, Volume 4, Issue 2.

retreat, listening to the words of inspirational speakers, dancing at a wedding, lighting Advent or Hanukkah candles, having a daily prayer time, or contemplating a sunset or a mountaintop view are all spiritual and religious practices undertaken by many of us in our daily lives. Some practices begin early in life, while others may be sought out in adulthood. What practices such as these have in common is the way in which they integrate different aspects of our human experience—our emotions with our intellect, or our minds with our bodies—while also connecting us with others who share similar beliefs.

Experiences such as these lift us out of our narrow selves and give us a glimpse, albeit temporary, of another way to view things as part of a larger picture. Spiritual and religious practices that help us integrate the body, mind, and spirit also provide psychological and physical benefits. There are many ways in which religion and spirituality impact health and well-being. Beginning with adolescence, rituals or rites of passage practiced by many of the major world religions play an important role in assisting individuals to successfully progress from one phase of life into the next. Most of these transitions, such as baptisms, circumcisions, confirmations, coming-of-age rituals, and marriages occur early in life.

What makes these religious traditions relevant to health, especially in adolescence and early adulthood, is that they provide rules for living. For example, some religions have very particular rules about diet and alcohol use, and most faiths have beliefs about maintaining the purity of the body as the vessel of the soul. In general, religious faiths discourage self-indulgent behaviours and promote moderation in all things. Many spiritual and religious practices involve the temporary and intermittent, or in some cases, lifelong denial of behaviours that are considered pleasurable by most people, such as drinking, eating meat, or having sex.

In a study called *Monitoring the Future*,[140] researchers from the University of Michigan analyzed data from an annual survey of high school seniors from 135 schools in 48 states. Their research findings show that religious involvement had a significant impact on the lifestyles of these students, especially in late adolescence. Students who said that religion was important in their lives and who attended religious services frequently, had lower rates of cigarette smoking, alcohol use, and marijuana use; higher rates of seat belt use, eating fruits, vegetables, and breakfast; and lower rates of carrying weapons, getting into fights, and driving while drinking. This is one of the few studies that has examined religiosity, spirituality, and health-related practices in adolescence. More importantly, these findings demonstrate the origins of a healthy adult lifestyle. Not smoking in adolescence, for example, dramatically reduces the likelihood that one will ever smoke. It also reduces the exposure to related risk factors that cause heart disease, cancer, and stroke, which all are major causes of death in our society.

A similar study of adults in Alameda County, California, also demonstrated that people who attend religious services are less likely to smoke cigarettes.[141] Moreover, findings from this study showed that those who attended religious services had lower mortality rates overall. It is not surprising that people who are less likely to

---

140 Wallace, J., & Forman, T. (1998). Religion's role in promoting health and reducing risk among American youth. *Health Education and Behaviour,* 25, 721–741.

141 Strawbridge, W. J., Cohen, R. D., Shema, S. J., & Kaplan, G. A. (1997). Frequent attendance at religious services and mortality over 28 years. *American Journal of Public Health,* 87, 957–961.

smoke, drink heavily, have casual sex with multiple partners, or get into fistfights, also have a longer life expectancy. In sum, there is ample evidence from well-designed population studies that religious and spiritual practices correlate negatively to some known health risk factors.

However, lifestyle factors are not the only mechanism that illustrates the relationship between religiosity and spirituality, and health and well-being. Another very important aspect of religious faith is that religious congregations become social circles, which provide support and reduce stress in people's lives. In 2008, the results of a nine-year longitudinal study of nearly 7,000 adults found that the most socially isolated people with the fewest social ties to others were at the highest risk of mortality.[142] One of the types of social ties these researchers included, along with family relationships, friendships, and community groups, was membership in a church or temple.

Social groups benefit not only because they provide rules for living, but also because social groups nurture, care for, and support their members. "Support" can be anything from helping out with tasks around the home when someone is sick to assisting someone in finding a new job, a dentist, or a day care provider. Or, it could mean having someone with whom to confide in and share feelings.

Religious congregations are excellent at providing social support for their members. A Duke University survey found that regular attendees at religious services reported larger social networks overall, more

---

142 Berkman, L. F., & Syme, S. L. (2008). Social networks, host resistance, and mortality: A nine-year follow-up study of Alameda County residents. *American Journal of Epidemiology*, 109, 186–204.

frequent telephone and in-person contact, and a stronger feeling of support from all the members of their social circles.[143]

Religious congregations are unique social institutions in that their membership cuts across the entire life cycle. No other social institution regularly brings together the very old and the very young and everyone in between. Additionally, religious congregations offer rich social resources with a strong sense of ethics. A core belief of each of the world's religious traditions is that of concern for others who are less fortunate and the deliberate turning of attention away from ourselves and toward others who are in need.

Spiritual and religious practices also offer us a transcendent time that the early twentieth century French sociologist Emile Durkheim called "*sacred time*"[144]. The experience of sacred time provides a time apart from the "*profane time*" in which we live most of our lives. A daily period of meditation, a weekly practice of lighting Sabbath candles or attending worship services, or an annual retreat in an isolated, quiet place of solitude—each of these are examples of setting time apart from the rush of our everyday lives. Periods of rest and respite from work and the demands of daily life serve to reduce stress, a fundamental cause of chronic diseases that are still the primary causes of death in Western society. Transcendent spiritual and religious experiences have a positive, healing, restorative effect, especially if they are built in, so to speak, to one's daily, weekly, seasonal, and annual cycles of living. Religiousness and spirituality have

---

143 Ellison, C. G., & George, L. K. (1998). Religious involvement, social ties, and social support in a southeastern community. *Journal for the Scientific Study of Religion*, 33, 46–61.

144 https://triumphias.com/blog/how-durkheims-idea-of-sacred-and-profane-be-used-to-understand-the-contemporary-society/

a cumulative effect on health across the life course that we may see most clearly only later in life.

Studies of mortality rates among Seventh Day Adventists, for example, show that the earlier the age of entry into the religious practice, the lower the mortality rate from cardiovascular disease.[145] Prevention of smoking, learning and practicing good dietary habits, getting regular exercise, setting time aside for rest and contemplation, being of service to others, and other important life commitments—established in adolescence—can reduce the risk for both chronic and infectious diseases over the entire life course. Thus, the cumulative effects of good health practices and social support facilitated by religious and spiritual practice can result in being physically and emotionally healthy.

But spiritual and religious practices are not, and should not be, seen solely as a means to an end when trying to achieve a healthier lifestyle. Spiritual and religious practices have their own intrinsic value and are sufficient ends in and of themselves. If there are side benefits or unintended consequences of those practices, while an interesting subject of study, it is not a sufficient reason for individuals to engage in such practices. Spirituality and religion centre around matters of ultimate concern that are of more importance than the health of our physical bodies and our day-to-day well-being. If such practices contribute positively to living healthier, happier lives—and it does appear they do—it is important that we know about it, and that research is undertaken to explore such relationships.

---

145 Fonnebo, V. (1992). Mortality in Norwegian Seventh-Day Adventists 1962–1986. *Journal of Clinical Epidemiology,* 45, 157–167.

Chapter Eight

Responding to Your Bounty of Blessings

Life is a series of choices. From the moment that we awake in the morning until the moment we nod off to sleep at night, we make countless decisions—decisions about the things we do (or fail to do), decisions about the words we speak (and the manner in which we speak them), and decisions about the way that we choose to direct our thoughts.

Life is a series of choices, each determining the trajectory that your life will take. Making choices in your life is very much like a journey. When you reach an intersection, or fork in the road, you choose which direction to take. That decision takes you down a path to other forks in the road and other decisions and choices. Each and every step of the way, your life is a series of choices.

So, as you pause to consider the kind of person you are and the kind of person you want to become, or the kind of person you want to be remembered as, ask yourself what kind of choices you tend to make in your day-by-day, moment-by-moment interactions with others. The choices are yours ... and so are the consequences. In retrospect, do your choices find you sitting on the fence or standing in the light? Are we for God, or are we not?

In sacred Scripture, in the Book of Joshua, we read of Joshua gathering all the tribes of Israel at Shechem, to renew their covenant with the Lord. It is an historical moment for the Jewish people because it was here, at Shechem, where God first appeared to Abraham, promising to make his descendants a great nation. It was here, at Shechem, where Jacob purchased land and settled his family. And it is here, at Shechem, where Joshua reminds the people that Yahweh has always been faithful to them. Joshua issues a blunt challenge to the people, saying, "*Choose this day whom you will serve*" (Joshua 24:15).[146] Either renew your covenant with God, or serve the pagan gods of the surrounding nations.

The "*pagan gods from beyond the river*," no doubt, had their attractions. The pagan gods probably demanded less and could be easily manipulated. But, Joshua's God, Yahweh, the God of Abraham, the God of Isaac, the God of Jacob, Joshua's God was more demanding. Joshua tells the people, "*As for me and my household, we ... will serve the Lord*" (Joshua 24:15).

For you and for me, the choice may not be so much about whether or not to be faithful to the Lord and to follow Jesus in our lives. We may have already made that decision. Instead, the decision for you and for me may be how we follow Jesus. Do we use the acronym, WWJD (*What would Jesus do?*) as the litmus test in the day-by-day, moment-by-moment decisions and interactions of our lives? Or do we follow the ways of the world? Do we live according to the flesh, or do we live according to the Spirit? How do we respond to a stranger

---

146 Holy Bible: New Revised Standard Version. (1993). Catholic Bible Press.

or a friend who is in need? Do we turn the other cheek when we are wrongly treated, or do we strike back; do we get even?

My brothers and sisters, with God's grace may we choose Jesus as completely and as unconditionally as He has chosen us.

This text, *Celebrate the Harvest*, is a reflection on the spiritual and religious life of older adults. With that analogy in mind, I offer six actions (and there are, no doubt, many more) that, as we advance in our years, we can utilize in response to the bounty of blessings which we have received throughout our lives. Those actions are:

1. Take stock of all that you have to offer

A few days ago, while I was waiting for an appointment, I picked up a newspaper that had been left on the seat next to me. It was folded open to the careers section, and the one that caught my eye read something like this: *"The successful applicant will be a dynamic, smart, take-charge individual who is able to bring an innovative perspective to management. Candidates must be creative thinkers possessing independent judgement and leadership, outstanding relationship-building skills, analytical ability, and the vision required to challenge employees and drive growth."*

I remember thinking that was a pretty tall order. I mean, really, who has the skill set to meet all those requirements? But some optimistic soul had circled the career opportunity in red. Someone looked at those words, at all those high expectations, and said, *"That's me! That's exactly who I am! I'm dynamic, smart, take-charge, talented, experienced, innovative, and creative! I'm an outstanding, analytical, visionary leader!"*

Of course, this talented, visionary, up-and-coming go-getter had left the paper behind in the doctor's office, so how bright could that person have been? I, at least, kept the paper.

In St. Paul's First Letter to the Church at Corinth, we have the job description for a Christian written by Christ and handed on by St. Paul. It's a pretty tall order, too:

> *Love is patient; love is kind; love is not envious or boastful or arrogant or rude. It does not insist on its own way; it is not irritable or resentful; it does not rejoice in wrongdoing, but rejoices in the truth. It bears all things, believes all things, hopes all things, endures all things* (1 Corinthians 13: 4–7).

We often hear this passage read at weddings. But here, St. Paul hands us the job description for a Christian. Not one of us is qualified for the position. Not one of us has the résumé for the job. But, that's okay, because St. Paul is challenging us to realize that it is only with Jesus that we can do these things which are expected. Left to our own devices, we do not have what it takes. On our own, all of our good intentions are exactly that—good intentions.

Paul's good news is that what we cannot do, God has already done in Jesus. We could not fit the job description, so God became human and through His life, death, and resurrection Jesus does what we cannot. Jesus equips us to be His disciples. He hires us as His apprentices.

Given that we are creatures of the flesh with all of it warts and bumps, we all grapple with sin. We all fall short. Perhaps, from time to time, we have eased into casual dishonesty or idle gossip. Perhaps we have been unwelcoming to the marginalized in our midst, or envious of the blessings which others have received, or have become experienced bearers of grudges. Perhaps we are impatient, quick to anger, or think unkindly of others.

How are we to gain victory over those sins of the flesh? If we have not already done so, we turn our lives over to Jesus Christ. We give Him the praise for every success, however small. We ask His forgiveness for every sin, however great. We leave off counting up our accomplishments, for nothing is ours except what Christ gives us.

In St. Paul's words of scripture, we are reminded of the purpose of the Christian job description, and that is eternal life with Father God. We begin that job in this life. We never become the manager. We are always interns, apprentices, and trainees. We have been hired not to lead, but to follow. We have been recruited to imitate, and to pray that through the endless mercy of the Father, our earthly work of following Christ may one day become an eternal career in heaven.

We enter this world at God's pleasure. He receives us when we leave. And He cheers for our success in between. He says, *"Follow my Son. Imitate him. He will walk beside you through each and every trial that life tosses in your path."*

Recently, my son Jeremy attended a music festival just outside of Slave Lake. As he arrived, his car got stuck in the muskeg. Shortly after, a fellow traveller got her car stuck very close to where Jeremy's vehicle was. Jeremy helped to push the woman's car out of the muskeg. And, in turn, some other Good Samaritans pushed Jeremy's car to safety.

Jesus's parable of the Good Samaritan gives us a name for all those people who step forward to help others. There are many of them around. Most of us have had the blessing of running into a Good Samaritan, a "neighbourly" person, a stranger who helped us to jump-start our car, who gave us directions when we were lost, or who went out of their way to be helpful.

When taking stock of all that you have to offer the world around you, keep that visual in mind. Put being a Good Samaritan high on your list of attributes. Our world would be cold, hard, and difficult without Good Samaritans.

2. Join in the harvesting

We read in the Gospel according to St. Matthew:

> *Then Jesus went about all the cities and villages, teaching in their synagogues, and proclaiming the good news of the kingdom, and curing every disease and every sickness. When he saw the crowds, he had compassion for them, because they were harassed and helpless, like sheep without a shepherd. Then he said to his disciples, "The harvest is plentiful, but the laborers are few; therefore, ask the Lord of the harvest to send out laborers into his harvest"* (Matthew 9:35–38).

This passage emphasizes the value of knowing the "field" in which we harvest and the responsibility we have in joining others in the fields harvesting, serving humanity, and when the opportunity arises, sharing our faith.

In the movie *Schindler's List*, one of the most moving scenes is near the end of the three-hour drama. Oscar Schindler invested his energy and his fortune in saving the lives of hundreds of Jews who would have otherwise been killed in Hitler's holocaust. Because the war is at its end, the Jewish people whom Schindler saved will become free men and women, while Schindler will become a fugitive. In the scene, Schindler walks to his car with his Jewish friend. Schindler begins to cry. He looks at his watch, knowing that if he had sold it, he might have saved another life. He looks at his car, knowing that he could have exchanged it for additional lives. Schindler says to his friend, *"I could have done more."*

I could have done more. Oscar Schindler knew he could have done more to save Jews from perishing in the death camps. In the same, but somehow less dramatic way, you and I can always do more to bring others to the Lord by our words, by our actions, and by our humanness.

Jesus did all he could. He *"went about all the cities and villages, teaching in their synagogues, and proclaiming the good news of the kingdom, and curing every disease and every sickness."* When He saw the crowds, the multitude of people, who needed to be saved from the eternal death camps, Jesus was moved. When you and I see the people as Jesus saw the crowds, and as Oscar Schindler saw the Jews in Nazi Germany, it will move us as well.

How did Jesus see the harvest?

- **The harvest is plentiful**

   The world is big. The crowds are huge. The number of people in need is overwhelming. In Jesus's day, the population of the world was approximately 150 million people. Today's world population grows 150 million every two-and-one-half years. Today, the world's population exceeds 7.8 billion people. Canada's population alone exceeds 38 million people.

- **The harvest is precious**

We read that when Jesus saw the crowds, He "*had compassion for them.*" The word used for compassion is the strongest word for pity in the Greek language. It describes the love that moves a person to the depths of their being. It is the type of love that moves people to cry for others, as Oscar Schindler cried for the Jews. It is love that moves people beyond sentimental feelings to heartfelt action.

- **The harvest is perplexed**

St. Matthew describes the crowd as being "*harassed and helpless, like sheep without a shepherd.*" Harassed means that they were defeated by life. The toils and struggles of life had punched them in the stomach one too many times. They are down for the final count, ready to quit. Helpless means they were broken and without purpose. They were wandering aimlessly. People without hope, without meaning, without a reason for living. Like "*sheep without a shepherd*" means they would follow any fad or guru or new idea, albeit to their own destruction.

In my everyday life, I don't often see sheep, but as I recall, sheep are weak, helpless, dependent creatures. If they are lost, they can't find their way home. If sick, they can't fight off disease. If threatened, they cannot run fast enough to escape danger. Sheep are crowd-followers. They simply put their heads down and follow the sheep in front of them. If a guide or leader does not exist, they will simply wander and wander and wander until they perish. When one panics—often for no real reason—the whole flock panics. They are timid, fearful, and curious. Come to think of it, that sounds a lot like me some days.

- **The harvest is perishing**

  In the Gospel according to St. John, we read where Jesus said to his followers, "*I tell you, look around you, and see how the fields are ripe for harvesting*" (John 4:35). Growing up on a Saskatchewan prairie farm, I know that ripened wheat takes on a golden hue when ready for harvest. However, if reaping is delayed, the heads will shatter, meaning that the grains will fall out onto the ground. As a result of the delay, the yield will be less profitable. Hence, there is always a sense of urgency to bringing in the harvest.

  My friends, we live in a lost and broken world that is desperate for the Good News of Jesus Christ. As followers of Jesus Christ, we have much work to do and little time to do it. The Gospel message is only good news if it arrives in time.

Herein lies one of the great truths of the Christian faith: The harvest will never be reaped unless there are those who are prepared to reap it. Jesus needs men and women like you and me to bring in the harvest. To do that, we need to see people as Jesus saw them, as plentiful, precious, perplexed, and perishing.

What can we do? We can take responsibility for our field. Think of all the people with whom you come in contact every day: family, friends, neighbours, the woman at the cleaners, the guy at the gym.

That is our field. We are responsible for them. We will never have a sense of urgency and priority until we realize that we are responsible for them.

We can pray. When we begin to see people as Jesus saw them, then we will pray for the harvest. We will pray for the salvation of the lost, for the church to be trainers of reapers, and for men and women to go into the fields to bring in the harvest. We will pray for workers, labourers, servers, and givers.

But we must do more than pray. We can go. When we see people as Jesus saw them, we will go into the fields. We can't bring in the harvest without first going into the fields. Our job is not to save the harvest—that's God's work. Our job is to tell people about the Lord of the harvest. It may be a bit cliché, but, the word "gospel" begins with "go." Without going, there is no knowing.

And, we can share our story. Witness is a powerful motivator. There are those in the church who believe that being a witness and sharing our story is somehow a form of proselytization. Not so. Some people say, *"I'll let my life be my witness."* By the way, if you are one of those people, how's that going for you? How many people have come to Christ because they watched your life?

We have taken the Great Commission and made it into the great omission. A subtle false teaching says we can be evangelical without being evangelistic. It has us believe that we go to church rather than go into the world.

But, you say, there are so many people. The harvest is so vast. The needs are so overwhelming. What difference can I make?

I am reminded of the story about an old man walking the beach at dawn, who noticed a young boy up ahead picking up starfish and flinging them into the sea. Catching up with the youth, the older man asked what he was doing. The answer was that the stranded starfish would die if left in the morning sun. *"But the beach goes on for miles, and there are millions of starfish,"* countered the old man. *"How can your effort make a difference?"* The young boy looked at the starfish in his hand, and then threw it to safety in the waves. *"It makes a difference to this one,"* he said.

I hope that your heart will be stirred to make a difference in the harvest. When we see people as Jesus saw people, it will draw us to join in the harvest, to take responsibility, to pray, to go and to tell about Jesus. And that, my friends, makes all the difference in the world.

3. Sort out the unusable fruit

In the Gospel according to St. John, we read one of the richest metaphors recorded in John's Gospel. It goes like this:

> *I am the true vine, and my Father is the vinegrower. He removes every branch in me that bears no fruit. Every branch that bears fruit he prunes to make it bear more fruit. You have already been cleansed by the word that I have spoken to you. Abide in me as I abide in you. Just as the branch cannot bear fruit by itself unless it abides in the vine, neither can you unless you abide in me. I am the vine, you are the branches. Those who abide in me and I in them bear much fruit, because apart from me you can do nothing. Whoever does not*

abide in me is thrown away like a branch and withers;
such branches are gathered, thrown into the fire, and
burned. If you abide in me, and my words abide in
you, ask for whatever you wish, and it will be done for
you. My Father is glorified by this, that you bear much
fruit and become my disciples (John 15:1–8).

Jesus says, "*I am the vine and you* [that's you and me] *are the*
branches." Jesus says, "*My Father, who is the vine grower, removes*
every branch that does not bear fruit." So, the expectation is that
we all bear fruit. But the reading sounds like it's going to hurt on
a regular basis even if we do bear fruit, because Jesus says that His
Father, the vine grower, prunes every branch that does bear fruit so
that it bears even more fruit.

For those of us who are not horticulturalists, Wilkinson, in his text,
Secrets of the Vine: Breaking Through to Abundance[147], provides an
excellent introduction. Wilkinson says that it's helpful to know
something about plant growth. Left to its own devices, a plant that is
growing naturally assumes the shape that allows it to make the best
use of light given the location and the climate.

The grapevine is no exception. Wilkinson points out that the
branches of a grapevine can become so dense that the sun can't
reach into the areas where fruit should form. Left to its own devices,
a grape plant will always favour new growth over more grapes. As a
result, from a distance, one can see a plant with luxurious growth, an
impressive sight indeed. But, up close, the result is an underachiev-
ing harvest. The result is little in the way of good fruit.

---

147 Wilkinson, Bruce (2001). Secrets of the Vine: Breaking Through to Abundance.
Multnomah Publishers. Oregon.

Because of the grape plant's tendency to grow so vigorously in a warm climate such as Israel, a lot of wood must be cut away, or pruned, each year. In fact, pruning the grape plant is the grower's best way of ensuring a plentiful harvest.

So, let's look at that passage one more time. Jesus says, "*My Father, who is the vine grower, breaks off every branch that does not bear fruit ... and He prunes every branch that does bear fruit.*" For the Christian, rapid and uncontrolled growth represents all those priorities and distractions in our lives, which while not wrong in and of themselves, are keeping us from significant ministry. They are keeping us from bearing bountiful fruit for God. Without the occasional pruning, we can live up to only a fraction of our potential, only a fraction of God's plan for our lives.

This principle of pruning invites a revealing question about our spiritual lives. If we are praying for God's abundant blessings, if we are pleading to be more like Jesus, then we are asking for God to prune us. For pruning is God's answer to our prayers so that our lives will be pleasing to Him that we might bear much fruit for the harvest.

There is hardly a passage in all the New Testament that better defines the nature of Christian discipleship. In this passage, Christ tells us what God wants from us, what God does for us, and what God expects of us.

First, Christ tells us what God wants from us. In a word, God wants fruit! Fruit is mentioned six times in this text and a total of eight times in this chapter. In the eighth verse, Jesus says, "*My Father is glorified by this, that you bear much fruit and become my disciples.*"

God wants us to bear fruit. But what kind of fruit are we called to bear? We're called to bear the fruit of Christian character and Christian conduct. Let's start with the fruit of Christian character. In St. Paul's Letter to the Galatians, he speaks of the fruit of the Spirit. St. Paul says:

> ... *the fruit of the Spirit is love, joy, peace, patience, kindness, generosity, faithfulness, gentleness, and self-control. There is no law against such things. And those who belong to Christ Jesus have crucified the flesh with its passions and desires. If we live by the Spirit, let us also be guided by the Spirit. Let us not become conceited, competing against one another, envying one another* (Galatians 5:22–26).

These are the qualities of Christian, or Christlike, character.

In his Letter to the Colossians, St. Paul says that we are called also to bear the fruit of Christian conduct. St. Paul says that we are to "*lead lives worthy of the Lord, fully pleasing to him, as you bear fruit in every good work and as you grow in the knowledge of God*" (Colossians 1:10). You see, Christian character produces Christian conduct. If we have the Spirit of Christ living in us, then He will produce Christlike conduct through us.

So, what can we reflect on today? First, think about the fruit which you are bearing. Is there room for improvement? Remember that most of us do bear good fruit. We may not even realize it.

Second, review what pruning is. It is a way to make things better, a way to make a better plant, a better tree, a better orchard. If you cut tired old branches from your rose bush, the plant doesn't wither.

No! It begins to thrive again. Pruning encourages new growth, and bigger and more beautiful blossoms begin to appear. Seen in this way, you and I do need to be trimmed from time to time, don't we? Pruned not as a means of punishment, but pruned as an opportunity to revitalize the spiritual health of the whole person, and ultimately the mystical body of Christ.

Finally, my brothers and sisters in Christ, take away from this message the need to trust in the steadiness and the purpose of God's gardening hand. Trust, even while suffering.

Then you can say to the Lord with unwavering faith: Go ahead, trim whatever gets in the way! For I am not the vine. I am the branch. My job is not to be perfect. My job is to remain in You, Jesus, and to let You do good within me and through me. Father God, prune from me whatever does not give life. And nourish within me whatever does give life.

May each of us bear fruit, more fruit, and much fruit for God's glory!

4. Celebrate the bounty

My family has been blessed with the opportunity to visit the Holy Land on two separate occasions, first in 2008, when I was discerning my call to the permanent diaconate, and then again in 2012. On one trip, as our vehicle ascended from the Sea of Galilee to what is called the Mount of the Beatitudes, I was reminded of St. Matthew's Gospel on the Parable of the Sower. The Gospel writer tells us:

> *That same day Jesus went out of the house and sat beside the sea. Such great crowds gathered around him that he got into a boat and sat there, while the whole*

crowd stood on the beach. And he told them many things in parables, saying: "Listen! A sower went out to sow. And as he sowed, some seeds fell on the path, and the birds came and ate them up. Other seeds fell on rocky ground, where they did not have much soil, and they sprang up quickly, since they had no depth of soil. But when the sun rose, they were scorched; and since they had no root, they withered away. Other seeds fell among thorns, and the thorns grew up and choked them. Other seeds fell on good soil and brought forth grain, some a hundredfold, some sixty, some thirty. Let anyone with ears listen!" (Matthew 13:1–9).

As I looked around at the barren landscape, which overlooks the Sea of Galilee, I saw rocky ground, footpaths, thorny bushes, and fertile areas. It reminded me that Jesus had no PowerPoint presentation to accompany His teachings. He used what was accessible to Him and His listeners—the landscape.

As one considers the landscape in the context of Jesus's words, the apparent paradox delivers a powerful teaching. By his actions, one would have thought that the sower in the parable was an amateur farmer. After all, what farmer would throw seeds on the rocks? Amongst the thorns? On the path? An experienced farmer would first clear the ground of rocks and stones, and gather the thorny bushes and have them burned. An experienced farmer would prepare the soil to receive the seed. And yet, the sower in the parable scatters seed wherever it may fall—on the rocks, amongst the thorns, on the footpath, and in the good soil.

Analogies have their limitations. However, if the sower in the parable is God, and the receiving ground is you and I, then the parable becomes even more powerful because of the folly of the sower. God is generous with His Word to the thorny ground and the rocky ground in equal measure, in the same way that He is generous with the fertile soil. God makes His grace available to everyone. The growth of the seed and the resultant harvest all depend on how the receiving ground chooses to respond. I am reminded that God does not expect me to be good soil first so that He can sow His seed deep within me. Rather, God sows His Word in me so that I might become good soil. I respond.

My response does not have to be a hundredfold all the time. It can be thirtyfold, sixtyfold, or hundredfold (Matthew 13:8). God still praises me, because I have played my part well enough. The workers in the vineyard who were hired at different times of the day did not all work for the same duration, and yet it was alright with the master (Matthew 20:1–16). All were equally rewarded. The servants who were given talents by their master did not all produce the same output (Matthew 25:14–30). And yet, each of those who produced something were praised and rewarded even more.

God wants us to open our hearts to willingly receive His Word. And He assures us they will not return to Him empty (Isaiah 55:11).

5. Give thanks

> *"The next footsteps in the corridor, he knew, might be those of the guards taking him away to his execution. His only bed was the hard, cold stone floor of the dank, cramped prison cell. Not an hour passed when he was*

free from the constant irritation of the chains and the pain of the iron manacles cutting into his wrists and legs. Separated from friends, unjustly accused, brutally treated—if ever a person had a right to complain, it was this man, languishing almost forgotten in a harsh Roman prison. But instead of complaints, his lips rang with words of praise and thanksgiving!"[148]

The man was St. Paul, a man who had learned the meaning of true thanksgiving, even during great adversity. Earlier, when he had been imprisoned in Rome, Paul wrote to the Church at Ephesus, with this direction:

> *... understand what the will of the Lord is. Do not get drunk with wine, for that is debauchery; but be filled with the Spirit, as you sing psalms and hymns and spiritual songs among yourselves, singing and making melody to the Lord in your hearts, giving thanks to God the Father at all times and for everything in the name of our Lord Jesus Christ* (Ephesians 5:17–20).

Lest a reader believe that St. Paul could not have intended to say "always," he elaborated in his Letter to the Colossians, saying, "*And, whatever you do, in word or deed, do everything in the name of the Lord Jesus, giving thanks to God the Father through him*" (Colossians 3:17). And, just in case the reader should question St. Paul's challenge to give thanks "for everything," he elaborated even further in his First Letter to the Church at Thessalonica, wherein he instructs his

---

148 Graham, Billy. (2017). *Billy Graham: How to be thankful in all things*. Billy Graham Evangelistic Association.

listeners to "*... give thanks in all circumstances; for this is the will of God in Christ Jesus for you*" (1 Thessalonians 5:18).

In an article titled, *"How to Be Thankful in All Things,"*[149] well-known American evangelist Billy Graham says that *"nothing turns us into bitter, selfish, dissatisfied people more quickly than a spirit of ingratitude ... an ungrateful heart. And nothing will do more to restore contentment and the joy of our salvation than a true spirit of thankfulness."*

In our world today, not unlike in the ancient world, ingratitude and thanklessness are far too common. Too often, we forget to thank others for all that they do. Common courtesy is scorned. Our so-called busyness gets in the way. We take for granted the ways that others help us. Above all, we fail to thank God for His blessings.

Thankfulness is the natural outflowing of a heart that is attuned to God. The psalmist declared, *"Sing to the Lord with thanksgiving"* (Psalm 147:7). A spirit of thanksgiving is always the mark of a joyous Christian. Why should we be thankful? Because God has blessed us, and we should be thankful for each and every blessing.

Billy Graham offers some of the reasons for which we should be thankful. They are:

- **Thank God for the material blessings that he gives you**

  We seem never to be satisfied with what we have, whether rich or poor, healthy or sick. But what a difference it makes when we realize that everything we have has been given to us as a pure gift by God. In his Letter to the Church at Philippi, St. Paul declared, *"I have learned to be content with whatever*

---

149 Graham, Billy. (2017). *Billy Graham: How to be thankful in all things.* Billy Graham Evangelistic Association.

I have. I know what it is to have little, and I know what it is to have plenty. In any and all circumstances I have learned the secret of being well-fed and of going hungry, of having plenty and of being in need. I can do all things through him who strengthens me" (Philippians 4:11–13).

Are you constantly preoccupied with what you do not have? Or have you learned to thank God for what you do have? A spirit of thankfulness makes all the difference.

- **Thank God for the people in your life**

It is easy to take people for granted, or to complain and become angry because they do not meet our every expectation. But we need to give thanks for those around us: our spouses, our children, our relatives, our friends, and those who help us in some way, as well as those who do not.

Do you let others know that you appreciate them and are thankful for them? The Christians in Corinth were far from perfect, but Paul began his first letter to them by saying, *"I give thanks to my God always for you because of the grace of God that has been given you in Christ Jesus"* (1 Corinthians 1:4). Thank God for all those who touch our lives in so many ways, great and small.

- **Thank God in the midst of trials and persecution**

We draw back from difficulties, yet not one of us is exempt from troubles in our lives. In many parts of the world, it is dangerous even to be a Christian because of persecution. And yet during those trials we can thank God, because we know that He has promised to be with us and that He will help us.

We know that He can use times of suffering to draw us closer to Himself.

In his Letter to the Church at Rome, St. Paul explains this point when he tells us that we are to *"boast in our sufferings, knowing that suffering produces endurance… and endurance produces character… and character produces hope… and hope does not disappoint us… because God's love has been poured into our hearts through the Holy Spirit that has been given to us"* (Romans 5:3–5).

I don't know what trials you may be facing right now, but God does. I don't know what heartaches you may be facing right now, but I do know that God loves you and is with you by His Holy Spirit. Cultivate a spirit of thankfulness even in the midst of trials and heartaches.

- **Thank God for His continued presence and power in your life**

At the commissioning of His disciples, Jesus told them, *"All authority in heaven and on earth has been given to me. Go therefore and make disciples of all nations, baptizing them in the name of the Father and of the Son and of the Holy Spirit, and teaching them to obey everything that I have commanded you. And remember, I am with you always, to the end of the age"* (Matthew 28:18–20).

We often tend to think that our Lord is present only in extraordinary ways or in our mountaintop experiences. But that thought could not be farther from the truth. Jesus is constantly present to us in very ordinary ways, such as:

- in the kind advice of a friend;
- in last evening's beautiful sunset;

- in the smile of a shopkeeper;

- in the jar of preserves or fresh garden produce that your neighbour dropped off this morning;

- in the laughs and the memories shared with your children when they called last evening;

- in the note that arrived unexpectedly from an acquaintance long forgotten;

- in the disease/cancer detection that almost did not happen due to an almost missed appointment;

- in the car trouble that caused you to avoid being part of that multi-vehicle pile-up on the highway.

And the list could go on and on for each one of us. In fact, every morning that God wakes us up is an example of His goodness. This means we are still working toward the purpose and gifts He has given us. It shows that He is not finished with us yet and that we still have a mission to fulfill. In the words of the prophet Isaiah, *"Morning by morning he wakens—wakens my ear as those who are taught"* (Isaiah 50:4).

In St. Paul's First Letter to the Church at Corinth, he asks, *"Do you not know that you are God's temple and that God's Spirit dwells in you?"* (1 Corinthians 3:16). Analogous to the Old Testament passages about the tabernacle, we find that the individual Christian is both the temple and the altar of divine presence. So, when we ask, where is Christ today, we can have only one response: that He is in each and every one of His faithful.

- **Thank God especially for His salvation in Jesus Christ**

  God has given us the greatest gift of all, His Son, who died on the cross and rose again so that we can know Him personally and spend eternity with Him in heaven. St. John tells us that, "*For God so loved the world that he gave his only Son, so that everyone who believes in him may not perish but may have eternal life*" (John 3:16). All we need to do is reach out in faith.

6. Set New Intentions

"*How can I know God's will in my life?*" That's a frequently asked question. Life is filled with tough decisions, and we sometimes find it hard to understand God's will in our lives.

It's been said that ninety percent of knowing God's will is using the wisdom that He has already given us. We find His wisdom throughout sacred Scripture. We learn from the nature and character of Christ. We learn from Church teachings. All of these provide an abundance of principles and values for knowing God's will.

We also learn from the prompting of the Holy Spirit, and from the doors which God opens and closes. God is more than willing to guide us in making decisions. All we need do is be willing to be guided.

Let's turn now to a couple of passages which provide strong examples for us on how it is that we come to discern God's will. Our first passage is taken from the First Book of Samuel.

> *Now the boy Samuel was ministering to the Lord under Eli. The word of the Lord was rare in those days; visions were not widespread. At that time Eli, whose eyesight had begun to grow dim so that he could not*

see, was lying down in his room; the lamp of God had not yet gone out, and Samuel was lying down in the temple of the Lord, where the ark of God was.

Then the Lord called, "Samuel! Samuel!" and he said, "Here I am!" and ran to Eli, and said, "Here I am, for you called me." But he said, "I did not call; lie down again." So he went and lay down.

The Lord called again, "Samuel!" Samuel got up and went to Eli, and said, "Here I am, for you called me." But he said, "I did not call, my son; lie down again." Now Samuel did not yet know the Lord, and the word of the Lord had not yet been revealed to him.

The Lord called Samuel again, a third time. And he got up and went to Eli, and said, "Here I am, for you called me." Then Eli perceived that the Lord was calling the boy.

Therefore, Eli said to Samuel, "Go, lie down; and if he calls you, you shall say, 'Speak, Lord, for your servant is listening.'" So Samuel went and lay down in his place.

Now the Lord came and stood there, calling as before, "Samuel! Samuel!" And Samuel said, "Speak, for your servant is listening" (1 Samuel 3:1–10).

Samuel discovered God's will regarding a specific situation by doing two simple things: he listened, and he responded to God's call. Twice Samuel heard God's voice and he responded by going to his mentor, Eli. Twice, Eli sent him back to bed. Then Eli gave Samuel some good advice. "If it happens again, say, '*Speak, Lord, for your servant is listening.*'" In other words, be still. Be still and listen for what God has to say.

Samuel was open to listen to God's promptings. As a result, Samuel became a key figure in Jewish history, ranking alongside Moses and King David.

The passage puts it in a very powerful and poetic way. It says, "*As Samuel grew up, the Lord was with him ... and let none of his words fall to the ground.*" In other words, Samuel continued to listen carefully to what God was saying. And, God continued to speak to Samuel.

Biblical writers know all about the human quest for God. But the Bible is not about our quest for God, it's about God's quest for us. We see it in the above scriptural passage as God pursues Samuel.

Next, let's turn to the New Testament, the Gospel according to St. John.

> *The next day John the Baptist again was standing with two of his disciples, and as he watched Jesus walk by, he exclaimed, "Look, here is the Lamb of God!" The two disciples heard him say this, and they followed Jesus.*

> *When Jesus turned and saw them following, he said to them, "What are you looking for?" They said to him, "Rabbi" (which translated means Teacher), "where are you staying?" He said to them, "Come and see." They came and saw where he was staying, and they remained with him that day. It was about four o'clock in the afternoon.*

One of the two who heard John speak and followed him was Andrew, Simon Peter's brother. He first found his brother Simon and said to him, "We have found the Messiah." He brought Simon to Jesus, who looked at him and said, "You are Simon son of John. You are to be called Cephas" (which is translated Peter). (John 1:35–42).

In this passage, we see Andrew and the other disciple discover Jesus and inquire after Him. How does Jesus respond? He engages them in conversation.

Here the disciples come running after the Lord, and Jesus turns and asks them a question. "*What are you looking for?*" What a powerful, thought-provoking question. "*What are you looking for?*" Jesus asks the disciples. Put yourself in the place of Andrew and the other disciple. Imagine the Lord standing right in front of you and He turns and He says, "*What do you want in your life? What are you looking for?*" My friends, let that question be your point of meditation this day.

What would you say? Very often in life, we kind of know what we want. We might want money, or power, or privilege, or friendships. But now, the Lord addresses you at the level of the heart. "*What are you looking for?*" How would you respond?

The disciples respond by answering with their own question. They ask, "*Rabbi ... where are you staying?*" Now that might sound peculiar. But you see, the disciples know that the deepest longing of their hearts is to stay with Him, to abide with Jesus. They want to know Jesus. And, Jesus responds: "*Come and see.*"

So, they went and spent time with Him, they stayed with Him that day. Then Andrew brought his brother Simon to meet Jesus.

Here is a great detail from our reading. St. John tells us that these things took place *"about four o'clock in the afternoon."* Nothing is incidental in sacred Scripture. John has a specific purpose for recording the time of day. As I referenced earlier in this text, for ancient Jews, numbers had great significance. John tells us *"it was about four o'clock in the afternoon."* Elsewhere, sacred Scripture tells us that Jesus died at three o'clock in the afternoon. And so, four o'clock designates what comes after Christ's crucifixion. It designates the time of the resurrection, which means, if you will, the time of Holy Mother Church.

The two disciples who come and stay with Jesus at four in the afternoon represent all of us. All of us Christian disciples who, down through the ages, will *come and see* and stay with the Lord. How do we stay with the Lord? How do we come to know Him and His will in our lives?

Like Samuel, we are moving in the right direction when we are still and listen for God's voice. Praying is first and foremost listening for Jesus. So, whatever you do with your life, keep on listening for the voice of Jesus. It comes in many ways—as a gentle voice in your heart, a song on the radio, the advice of a friend. Like Samuel, we are moving in the right direction when we respond with a willing heart. *"Here I am, Lord. I come to do your will."*

Like Andrew, we are moving in the right direction when we abide with Jesus, when we spend quality time with Him in public and private worship, in meditative reading and Bible study, in personal and family prayer, in works of mercy, and in the sacraments and the sacred Liturgy. Like Andrew, we are moving in the right direction when we share our experiences with others, when we bear witness for Christ, sharing the Good News of love, and peace, mercy, and forgiveness. Sharing what we have seen and heard and experienced and then inviting others to *"come and see."* That's how we come to know God's will for our lives.

Don't worry, my friends, if at first you don't hear God's voice. As He did with Samuel, God is a loving and persistent Father who continues to call you by name. The Lord holds us in the palm of His hand as we journey through this life. And He reaches out to embrace us as He welcomes us home in the next.

Let us pray:

> May the Lord bless you and keep you;
> May the Lord make his face to shine upon you,
> and be gracious to you;
> May the Lord turn His face towards you,
> and give you peace.
>
> And, may the blessing of God Almighty,
> Father, Son and Holy Spirit,
> be among you and remain with you always.
>
> Amen.

Appendix

Data Sources

Research Study[150]

In completing the requirements for a Masters in Health Administration with a specialty in Long Term Care, I designed a quantitative study to determine whether selected demographic, social, and health related characteristics influence the older adult's perceived fulfillment of his/her spiritual needs. As well, this study sought to identify those characteristics which contribute to explaining the older adult's reported level of spiritual need fulfillment.

The data for this study was collected by way of a comprehensive questionnaire, which I designed for the specific purpose at hand. Eight categories of independent variables were analyzed to determine their relationship to the dependent variable, which was spiritual need. In addition, five demographic variables were tested. They included age, gender, marital status, nationality, and religious affiliation.

---

150 Bell, W. C. (1989) *Celebrate the harvest: A study of the spiritual needs of the older adult.* M.H.A. University of Minnesota. Twin Cities Health Sciences (Bio-Medical) Library WT145 B435c 1989.

Portions of the survey tool were patterned after the Salamon-Cote Life Satisfaction of the Elderly Scale (LSES). LSES enjoyed the enviable position of having met accepted standards for withstanding the tests of validity and reliability. In order to secure face validity of the survey tool, I sought the input of a number of Christian and Jewish religious who were seen as being experts in the field of spiritual needs. The religious consulted were also experienced in assessing and caring for the spiritual needs of older adults.

The target population for purposes of this study was a random sample of the Saskatchewan population. For logistical purposes, it was necessary to restrict the population to be studied to a single province rather than seeking to survey a random sample of the entire Canadian older adult population.

Data was collected by way of a mail questionnaire, with responses provided by a randomly selected sample of older adults in the province of Saskatchewan. The sample population of older adults was secured with the support of Saskatchewan Health. The Information Systems Branch of Saskatchewan Health drew the random sample of survey-eligible participants from amongst those health beneficiaries who were registered on the province's Health Insurance Registration File (HIRF). Consistent with departmental policy, the names and addresses of beneficiaries were released to, and mailed out by, an independent, arms-length third party, in my case, the Continuing Care Branch of Saskatchewan Health. Appropriate safeguards were incorporated into the study design to ensure respondent anonymity.

For testing each of the hypotheses, I used the Statistical Package for the Social Sciences (SPSS)[151] and the services of the computer centre at the University of Minnesota.

Literature Review

A literature review is a comprehensive summary of what has been published on a topic by accredited scholars and researchers. The review surveys scholarly articles, books, and other sources relevant to a particular area of research. It seeks to enumerate, describe, summarize, objectively evaluate, and clarify this previous research and thereby provide a theoretical base for the research at hand. A literature review creates a "landscape" for the reader, providing a full understanding of the developments in the field. This landscape informs the reader that the author has indeed assimilated all (or the vast majority of) previous, significant works in the field into her or his research.

The literature review for the original study was focused on research related to the meaning of spirituality and the spiritual needs relative to older adults in particular. It should not be assumed that spirituality is either synonymous or coterminous with religion. It is suggested that to adopt this restrictive view is unhelpful in the provision of individualized care.

Reflection on the literature reveals that the self, others, and our Supreme Being provide the key elements within a definition of

---

151 SPSS Statistics is a well-respected software package used for interactive, or batched, statistical analysis. In addition to statistical analysis, data management (case selection, file reshaping, creating derived data) and data documentation (a metadata dictionary is stored in the data file) are features of the base software.

spirituality, and that other emerging themes, namely meaning, hope, relatedness/connectedness, beliefs/belief systems, and expressions of spirituality can be articulated in the context of those three key elements. In particular, it is proposed that the nature of God, or a Supreme Being, may take many forms, and essentially is whatever an individual takes to be of highest value in his or her life. It is suggested that the themes emerging from the literature can be utilized as a framework to give practitioners and researchers a direction for future exploration of the concept of spirituality and spiritual need.

In preparation for writing this text, a second comprehensive literature review was conducted. This latest literature review examined recent published research in reference to the meaning of spirituality and spiritual need particularly as it relates to the older adult population. This latest review also investigated research related to the religious practices of older adults.

Personal Experience

In addition to the correlational study and an extensive literature review, I bring a lifetime of clinical experience in health services, specifically serving the unmet needs of older adult populations. I hold academic preparation in psychiatric nursing, health services administration, administration of services for older adults, public policy, and the permanent deaconate. Throughout my career, using the knowledge gained from each of those academic streams, I have been blessed with innumerable opportunities to serve older adult populations, both individually and in cohorts, and to influence service systems affecting that population.